The Mystic Philosophy of Sant Mat

The Mystic Philosophy of Sant Mat

Peter Fripp

RADHA SOAMI SATSANG BEAS
PUNJAB, INDIA

Published by:
Shri S. L. Sondhi, Secretary
Radha Soami Satsang Beas
Distt. Amritsar, India

First edition 1964 2,500 copies
Second edition 1978 (revised) 5,000 copies
Third edition 1987 5,000 copies

Printed at India Offset Press, Mayapuri, New Delhi-110064

HUZUR MAHARAJ SAWAN SINGH (1858-1948)

SARDAR BAHADUR JAGAT SINGH MAHARAJ (1884-1951)

MAHARAJ CHARAN SINGH—The Present Master

BELOVED SATGURU

The following pages, which are but the threshold of Sant Mat, are the humble expressions of gratitude my wife and I feel for inestimable privileges.

CONTENTS

LIST OF ILLUSTRATIONS

FOREWORD

HQ Eastern Air-Command,
Indian Air Force,
Rani Kutir, Regent Park,
Calcutta–40.

In this world of constant change, apparently accelerated in our time by unprecedented scientific and technological achievements, exaltation of man and his material progress is the outstanding theme. It is to our "supremacy" and ever increasing control over the forces of nature, to our standards of physical existence and social and cultural pursuits that we continue, more than ever, to devote all our thoughts and efforts. We see, and perhaps strive only to see and enjoy but one side of the picture, as it were—the picture of the phenomenal sensual world.

Great saints and masters of all ages have pointed to the other side of the picture—the reality not subject to change—and in their tender mercy, have offered those that would care to follow their lead to show the way in a positive and practical manner, which no mere reading of scriptures could equal. They have proclaimed the true supremacy of man as being the highest form of creation, having alone the capacity to make contact with his Creator, if he would, and solving the eternal mystery during his lifetime.

This book is about the philosophy of the Saints, about the inner path along which the soul must travel to reach its ultimate destiny, about the indispensability of a living Master and about the duties of a true disciple. It is meant only for the honest seeker, that is, one who is interested in pure spiritual uplift in the literal sense without any thought of physical and material benefits. Sant Mat is not a new religion; it is a philosophy which gives practical shape to the truth common to all contemporary religions.

Peter Fripp, the author of this book, whom I greatly respect and admire as a friend, has very ably presented all aspects of this philosophy for the guidance mainly of Western readers. I hope they will not fail to profit by it.

1964

K. L. SONDHI
Air Vice-Marshal

PROLOGUE

"Maharaj Ji, I know that intellectual hair-splitting is useless, yet again and again these questions arise in my mind—why did God create the Universe, why did He send us down from Sach Khand, why does He allow so much misery to prevail in this world, and so on."

The Great Master said, "I will ask Dr. Johnson to tell you a story I related to him a few days ago. It may amuse and interest you."

. . . The story was about a blind man who fell into a deep well. A man happened to pass that way and, taking pity on the sad condition of the blind man, offered to pull him out. For this purpose, he dropped one end of a long rope into the well and asked the blind man to catch hold of it, so that he could be pulled out.

Instead of taking hold of the rope, however, the blind man started a long and senseless harangue about how he had fallen into such a deep well, why the good man wanted to take him out, what his motive might be in thus helping him and what guarantee did he have that he would not fall into some other well as soon as he was out.

The patience of the kind rescuer was taxed heavily by all this nonsense, but he calmly replied that it would be in the blind man's best interest to take advantage of the rope now, and after he was out, he could study the situation at leisure.

But once again the blind man started to ramble on, asking how it was that the man with the rope had not himself fallen into a well. The rescuer then told him he had other important tasks to attend to, so he would have to leave the blind man in the well if he did not come out within a few minutes.

"Alright," said the blind man. "But first please tell me, how deep is this well, and when was it built?"

"Well, it's deep enough to be the grave of many like you," said the rescuer and went his way.

We all laughed at the folly of the blind man, and then the Great Master said, "Isn't this exactly what we all do? Actually, our intellect and reasoning sometimes become great hindrances in the way of our release."

Adapted from
Call of the Great Master
by Daryai Lal Kapur

1

LISTENING TO INAUDIBLE MUSIC

A PRELUDE

In this restless world, the demands made by the feverish tempo of present day life and the constant straining of the resources of mankind, both mental and physical, create more problems than solve the old ones. True, we live longer, but our faster pace of living presents us with more and more crises that leave little time for quietude and listening. Indeed, relaxation is so unusual that the very word "relax" has become a kind of half-humorous catchword. Too often, it is induced by drugs and tranquilisers, with the disastrous result that the main object of life is missed because of dulled perception. In addition, we allow the true purpose of life to be buried under an avalanche of urgent but disconcerting material considerations. This intense involvement with material things leaves us without the consolation of peace, contemplation, or the pursuit of higher aspirations. Indeed, the very words "higher aspirations" would appear to indicate only bigger doses of the same thing—that is, higher standards of living or material comfort—and "peace" seems to be only a state of cold war or perhaps a brief breathing space between crises.

But the pendulum swings, and many people, acutely aware of a spiritual vacuum, are recoiling from the great callousness of human behaviour that is so astonishingly exhibited even in this twentieth century. The vociferous so-called demands for freedom more often than not end in unbridled license and in sheer caricature of a great ideal. Overflowing hospitals, clinics, prisons and reformatories belie most of our claims of progress. We can scarcely congratulate ourselves upon this unhappy state of affairs. On the contrary, it calls even more loudly than before for a deep reassessment of the human situation and all its accepted values. It is fairly obvious that we must be overlooking a vital factor. To find what it is we must start from the beginning, and this is self-discovery.

We are passing into a new phase of unfoldment. Therefore, the essentially valid question may be, indeed must be, asked once more: what is the purpose of life, and what kind of a practical man fulfills that purpose? Is he essentially a materialist, or is he perhaps something of a mystic? It is a searching, challenging question, but a very great authority—Maharaj Charan Singh, a present day saint of whom we shall speak later—gives us some valuable guidance. He says of the materialist versus the mystic that the one is fascinated by the structure of created things, the other seeks knowledge of the Creator himself. A beautiful evaluation, but he does not leave us there. He freely gives us his whole teaching, the philosophy of Sant Mat (teachings of the saints), which is completely relevant to our problems. It is essentially a discipline for the practical mystic.

An out-and-out materialist, or even an intellectual who thinks of himself as a practical man, often finds it difficult to be patient with the idealist or dreamer of dreams. He forgets that truth is perhaps the other way around from what he perceives, that the things he handles at the material, three-dimensional level are but the outcome of the so-called dreamer's work. Indeed, it could be reasonably insisted that these evanescent material things and passing events are shaped and projected from a different level, one that is much higher than the phenomenal plane of the familiar but unreliable five senses.

Great authorities of many religions proclaim again and again that this is so. The Christian New Testament says that through the Word "all things were made." The Adi Granth, the bible of Sikhism, says the creation came out of "Nam." The Hindu Vedas say that out of the "Breath of Brahm" was everything made that was made. These scriptures clearly indicate that there is much more than just plain materialised (created) existence. Since you cannot get something out of nothing, it follows that there is another realm from which this physical, three-dimensional world was projected.

It behoves us, therefore, as practical men to find out exactly what is meant by those mysterious phrases "the Word," "Nam," and the "Breath of Brahm," for they are obviously three synonymous terms for a crucial matter from three different recognized authorities, and there are many more like them from other sources.

But personal investigation of the Word, the source of creation, the fountain of man's activities and aspirations, other than along material lines, is often thought to be dull and inconclusive. To be sure, it is interesting enough to speculate on these things or to hear them discussed in lectures on philosophy, theology and such, but if the search is adopted as a way of life, that is a different matter. It is then often seen as some sort of escapism or physiological upset, or something that interferes with the business and the reality of life. This is unfortunate because this investigation is by far the most important reality of life. And like any other study, it requires special technique, special terminology and special thought. It is tremendously absorbing work and infinitely rewarding. Its true significance, however, depends very much upon how it presents itself to one's mind, upon how deeply one enters, quite literally, into the spirit of it and, of course, upon what one finds *is* the business of life.

To make this search, we are singularly ill-prepared in spite of the existence of so many established religions and philosophies. If religion consists mostly of the observance of moral precepts, rituals and rules of thumb, however strictly obeyed, it gets nowhere. If philosophy consists of book studies, lectures and pious platitudes, it is indeed sterile.

From childhood onwards we are taught many things that sound most improbable and are hard to believe, but we accept them for the moment in good faith, even if with reservation and puzzlement. When we have grown enough to test these teachings, we often let them pass unchallenged as gospel truth, and they are automatically adopted as facts, rituals and conventions. But there comes a time when these ritualistic observances must be substantiated. Good faith must be implemented by mystic inner experiences of a personal and transcendental nature, or the truth of our beliefs must forever remain illusory.

But how is it possible to gain the mystic experiences that are, in essence, the sole reason for religions of all kinds? The Bible tells us that we are the highest form of creation, but it also says that we "have eyes, but do not see" and "ears, but do not hear." By good fortune, this situation can be rectified through the catalytic philosophy of Sant Mat. This philosophy gives a new and revivifying perspective to all religions and schools of philosophic thought. It offers direct experience of realms beyond the ordinary material plane, and it instructs one in how to achieve this experience.

This can be accomplished by listening to what we "do not hear," a special inner music that has a very special purpose. Sant Mat teaches one to listen to this inaudible music by a special practice called the yoga of the creative Sound Current or Divine Melody, or, in Hindi, Surat Shabd Yoga. This practice establishes a real platform for freedom and happiness of the highest order.

A great teacher of Sant Mat, Maharaj Sawan Singh Ji, of whom we shall also speak later, said in his *Discourses on Sant Mat*:

> Feeling instinctively that the earth is not his Home, man has been investigating restlessly to try to make a true appraisal of his predicament in this "Isthmus of a middle state," and to discover his real Home. Two principal methods have been adopted

by him for this purpose: one of science and the other of religion. Scientists seeking for truth outside the body, have delved into the earth, flown in the sky, crossed the mountains, reached the poles and formed some idea (even though their conceptions go on changing from age to age) of the nature and formation of the earth. They have not, however, discovered the Ultimate Truth by their investigations and have no inkling at all of our True Home. As a matter of fact, even modern philosophy, borrowing indiscriminately from modern science, has moved further from the truth by emphasizing the material aspect of the mind and the mechanical nature of the body.

But the second group of investigators, whom we call Saints, Perfect Masters, Mystics and Prophets has found a complete answer to man's query about his real Home. Working with much finer instruments and on higher planes, they have made remarkable discoveries which the world is as yet far from appreciating fully. A most wonderful fact is that their researches, conducted within the human body, which is itself a natural laboratory, have yielded similar results in all ages, climes and countries. They have rent the veils of illusion and have discovered truths that are eternal and immutable. In their books (which we call scriptures) they have left details of the inner spiritual journey. Now let us find out what they have to say about our True Home and the Path that leads to it.

The analysis of the self, as given by the Saints, reveals that there are three separate entities in man: the physical body, the mind and the spirit. The essence or real man is the soul or spirit, while the mind and body are accretions that the soul has acquired during the course of its endless wanderings. This earth is the home of the physical body alone (we have two other bodies, the astral and the causal, but these belong to higher realms). The home of the

> mind is in Trikuti (the second Heaven) whereas the home of the soul is in the highest of heavens called by Swami Ji as Radha Swami Dham, meaning "Abode of the Lord of the soul."
>
> ...The university of the spirit has its own teachers whom we call Masters and requires the same constant application as is needed for winning academic honours.

The way of attaining mystic experiences is summarized by the present spiritual Master of Sant Mat, Maharaj Charan Singh. It strikes a strange and unfamiliar note to the Western ear, for he says: "First comes the Grace of God, then the company of Saints and then the acquisition of the secret of Nam. Then, by constant application and unceasing devotion, comes the actual realization of Nam. That is the order." "Once started on the Path," he says, "we go on at our own pace according to our zeal and fervour for God-realization, and the debts of karma which we still have to discharge."

For a person who seriously wishes to reassess the human situation, this statement holds the key that opens the door of all deeper aspiration. For the actual realization by personal experience of the creative sound (or Word or Nam) is the mainspring, the common denominator of all true spiritual experience, and there is no simpler nor more direct approach to the experience than through Sant Mat philosophy. It is the basic truth of all religious doctrines in their highest aspect.

The "constant application and unceasing devotion" needed to realize the Word refers to the exercise of meditation and contemplation. Meditation is to still the mind by repetition and, when that is accomplished, to listen to that ensuing Word or creative Sound Current that is mentioned in practically all the scriptures of the world as the most vital factor. Contemplation is to observe and experience that which is revealed when the mind is stilled. Instruction on attaining access to the Sound Current in meditation is given by the living Master.

The whole of Sant Mat practice, as taught by the Masters, is designed to lift the attention of the mind far above the level at which dogmas have any significance, to where the theological barriers cease to exist. But the acceptance of this fact is essentially a personal act. An earlier Master of Sant Mat, Swami Ji of Agra, very wisely says:

> People become offended when advice is offered. One should, therefore, be careful before beginning conversation, and should not be persistent if anyone does not accept his views; nor should any attempt be made to convince the other person.
>
> *Sar Bachan*

However, we are not offended by advice that is offered with poetic beauty:

> Speak to Him, thou, for He hears, and
> Spirit with Spirit can meet—
> Closer is He than breathing, and nearer
> than hands and feet . . .
> And the ear of man cannot hear, and the
> eye of man cannot see;
> But if we could see and hear this Vision—
> were it not He?
>
> *The Higher Pantheism,*
> Alfred Lord Tennyson

Sant Mat delves deeply into the actual science of

hearing and seeing. Indeed, it is devoted to that end. Maharaj Sawan Singh says:

> This Word is not, as is usually believed, a written word. Actually, it is a power that emanates continuously from the Supreme Being, the Power that created and now sustains the vast universe of universes. The Saints and Perfect Masters teach their disciples how to contact this power, which is everywhere present . . . and is heard by initiates as the most enchanting and enrapturing harmony or melody. This music is not only beautiful, it is also purifying and uplifting. It purifies the human mind, and then draws the soul upwards with an irresistible Power—the Power of Love of the Supreme God Himself.
>
> *Discourses on Sant Mat*

This then is the way in which the endless round of incarnation is broken—karma is finished, laid aside—and reunion is eventually made with the Beloved, our Father the Absolute.

2

A PERSONAL JOURNEY

Like most people who had endured one or two wars with their indescribable horrors, or who had realized the hollowness of armchair idealism and platform speculations, both my wife and I were hungry for substantiation of many of the old statements—religious and philosophic—by personal experience. So it happened that one evening in 1954 my telephone rang and the voice of a stranger told me of a mutual friend who had suggested we should meet each other. It seemed he thought we had many things in common. This is always an intriguing situation to follow up, which of course we did.

We had indeed a great deal more in common than we at first expected. We were both deeply interested in metaphysical religion and philosophic outlook, and in India. Both were vegetarians, and, strange to say, both had attended the same school (Berkhamstead) at the same time fifty years before. This new contact was with one Colonel C. W. Sanders, late of the Indian Army.

For many years my wife Ann and I had read with delight most of the contemporary and often over-romantic novels touching on the fringes of Eastern mystic life, such as *Bengal Lancer*, *Garden of Vision* and *Lost Horizon*. We had always sensed the existence of an elusive but profound truth, but here was someone who had gone beyond the official army and a social way of life and had immersed himself deeply in the very world we had so lovingly read about but had never dared hope to experience personally.

In spite of army duties, the Colonel had been for some eighteen years a disciple of a great Guru (master or teacher), Maharaj Sawan Singh of the Punjab, India. Indeed, he was a very devout pupil, for he had brought the philosophy of Sant Mat to England with his book, THE INNER VOICE

I personally have had many interesting psychic experiences both in war and peace. Together and between us, my wife and I had explored many fascinating angles of thought—Mme. Blavatski with Mrs. Besant in theosophy, Dr. Steiner, Krishnamurti, Ouspenski and others. For me the search also included the ancient art of Freemasonry, which points out that the genuine esoteric knowledge and meaning of life has been lost by man's passions, yet can somehow, somewhere be regained at a mysterious centre.[1] (Had not the poet Milton amongst many others declared this?)

Always in these studies, our attention was directed towards the East. Here at last in Sant Mat was

[1]A number of crusaders to the Holy Land were captured or otherwise detained in the Near East and learned from the wise men (magi or gurus) the meaning of inner transport, which had been lost to men but which could be restored to them by a living Master. This was the basis of Freemasonry and other esoteric bodies, most of which endeavoured to translate these teachings into the Christian ethic. They then became immersed in ritual, thereby losing once more their essential esoteric and universal purpose. In its place they substituted symbols and pageantry.

a profound teaching, referring to that same central cortex, that was understandable and most inspiring and that, for me, did not invalidate Christianity or other approaches. On the contrary, it coordinated and brightly illuminated them. Without formalities, without rituals, without officials, temples or churches and without difficult yogic postures or complicated breathing techniques, here was something that appeared both practical and transcendental. And it was offered with the greatest simplicity by a living Master, a Saint, a Satguru.

How did we know, you may ask, that he was indeed a Satguru, a true Master? The truth is, of course, that we did not; but we were invited to listen, to read and to investigate the teaching thoroughly before arriving at conclusions.

It was some months before the Master graciously accepted us as pupils, but those intervening months proved to be the culmination of our studies to date, and many fateful things followed, all pointing in one direction. My professional life came to a close, together with the end of my lease and the maturing of insurances, all practically inviting us to a new state of activity; so that, wistfully expectant, we wrote for permission to visit India at the Radha Soami Satsang in the eastern Punjab. This small colony, which sits on the banks of the River Beas (where Alexander the Great ended his invasion eastward) with the Himalayas appearing in the distance, was soon to become to us much more than a dreamland or a Shangri-la.

There are many significant sidelights to a search for truth. Like most seekers, I have often been expectantly asked for gifts of money or invited to join something with a subscription. On this occasion the Master—called by some loving title such as Maharaj Ji or Huzur, or Satguru Ji, and who personally answers all letters from his vast following—replied, much to our surprise, that it was not necessary for us to travel so far or to bear so much expense. We could practise the teaching effectively wherever we found ourselves. If, however, we still wished to meet him personally, we would be most welcome. Naturally we went post haste, and in the course of many months, and after many requests, we were allowed to pay a very modest contribution towards our food and servant only. Also, to our surprise and great comfort, arrangements were made by him for us to be met at airports and railway stations in India by his disciples, and finally to be escorted into his presence in the Radha Soami Colony.

This was a very different matter from the romantic novels; our Master was so very real and his work was concerned in a very practical way with souls—ours and those of others who sought him. He was not an intangible entity such as we had often heard of in mystic teachings, an ascetic hidden away in the impenetrable hills whom no one ever contacted and whose work was vaguely mysterious. Our Master made mysticism a reality and working profundity.

It would be impossible to know what impression we two spiritual babes in the woods made upon Maharaj Ji at that meeting, but Ann and I both felt strangely at home and yet were in some way embarrassed. But the Master has command of all situations—as we found out not only then but also a thousand times since—and he soon gave us our bearings, so much so that the projected short visit was prolonged into eight months.

They were months of joy when the Master was with us, but of strange lifelessness when he was away teaching elsewhere over the wide stretches of the Indian subcontinent. When he went to nearby villages to give satsang (a meeting with a discourse), we were often enough invited to accompany him in his car and, on one occasion, to stay with him at his ancestral farm in Sikandarpur near Sirsa, some 200 miles to the south. Usually there are a number of Western disciples visiting the Dera, or resting place, as the colony is called, but for part of our stay, we were the only two and were therefore especially privileged.

During these eight wonderful months, we were delighted to wear Indian dress, which is remarkably comfortable and appropriate in hot weather, to eat the excellent local food and to live as nearly as possible in the Indian rhythm.

We were fortunate to be without radio, television, telephone or newspapers,[1] all of which "deprivation" was replaced by close interchange with other satsangis (disciples of Sant Mat). At the times of the biggest gatherings (bhandaras), which occurred four times yearly and lasted for several days of teaching and initiations, there would be anything up to two hundred thousand souls, in spite of the fact that the colony is twenty-five miles from any city[2] and three miles from a main road or rail. These vast audiences would include a generous cross-section of Indian life—princes,

[1]All these amenities are now available at the Dera.
[2]Amritsar is twenty-five miles away, Jullundur twenty-four miles.

army officers, businessmen and peasants—coming from all over India and speaking many languages. They were all fed without charge, served by voluntary help working day and night, but I never really discovered how the colossal and seemingly impossible task was accomplished. Throughout these huge and colourful gatherings there were never any police present and no incidents.

In the normal life of all Indian spiritual centres and ashrams there is a more or less continuous movement, in and out, of passing sadhus, *sanyasis*, yogis and other mystics and holy men, and it is possible to contact many divergent views. At different times there came two *sanyasis*, very learned and practised in Raja Yoga and, fortunately for me, also well enough versed in English.

One of them, the younger of the two, was quite sure that he and I had met in the past, and my own feelings were reciprocal, for it was I who singled him out amongst a vast crowd. He was a remarkably dapper, well-groomed man who obviously had not entirely renounced the world in spite of his orange robe. It seemed that he was prideful of his spiritual powers, and in many ways he indicated that he lived on the fat of the land. He told me after a few days at the colony that he was not impressed. He felt quite sure that the Master had nothing to teach him, and he tried to convert me to Raja Yoga, of which the present Master, Maharaj Charan Singh, says:

> Hatha Yoga, I may point out, is an excellent discipline for the body. Raja Yoga is better but that too does not enable you to control the mind *fully* nor does it finish your series of births and deaths, for the *seeds* of karma are not destroyed by that method.

> Surat Shabd Yoga enables you to "roast" the seeds of karmas, as it were, so that they cannot sprout again. Mind can only be fully controlled by a Power which has its origin beyond the mind, and that is the Divine Sound.
>
> *Light on Sant Mat*

One morning while Ann and I were walking on the river bank, we passed him and a companion. I greeted him with our salutation of "Radha Soami," which means "Lord of the soul." He replied with a sonorous "Aum," and I felt a strong emanation like a small blast of wind. Then he passed along on his wanderings and beggings and I knew him no more.

But the other *sanyasi*, an older, I think, wiser man, stayed to experience a different fate. He had been to England and knew the Lake District quite well, so we had some common ground. We had many talks, some serious and some light-hearted, on the river bank and in the compound. When I had made real companionship with him, he confessed that he had heard of the Master's teaching and had come armed with his yogic power to demand whatever it was the Master had and he had not.

Strangely enough he did not receive entry to the Master's presence. Day after day for weeks, at first expectantly and then doggedly, he waited outside the gates of the Master's garden. Gradually I saw the arrogance fade into perplexity, and then into downright humility. He begged a hot bath from our *chowkidar* (caretaker), the first, he said, for years.

A few more days and suddenly his air of dejection changed to one of joy and sparkle. He had been invited in and had met and talked with Maharaj Ji.

He had changed into a pure white Punjabi suit, and the last we saw of him, he was setting out to earn his living—without his begging bowl.

The Master is not enamoured of laziness or dilettantism. It is a rule that every disciple must earn his own livelihood unless retired or disabled. Even many retired men are honoured to be main supports in the work of the colony. At the time of our sojourn, there were a professor of languages, an ex-banker, two retired judges, a professor of agriculture, doctors of medicine, ex-teacher and a minister of the church.

All of our encounters in the colony made us focus on the spiritual side of life. When a few kindly friends in the West, feeling that we were unduly isolated, forwarded bundles of newspapers, the shock of their seeming brashness and vulgarity, after the exercise in serenity, was so great that we felt impelled to dispose of them, which we did. This may sound smug, but it was a very sincere and natural reaction.

This is not to suggest that all India is saintly, far from it. The mysterious East is becoming speeded up—to its material benefit. The twentieth century has even obtruded itself on the colony, which has lately been obliged by the new tax and land laws of India to form itself into a society in order to maintain and develop sufficient land for its growing requirements. But there are still a few of the old caves for meditation high up in the river banks, so carefully tended and so clean, that had fascinated one Western disciple so much he ordered one to be made for himself.

It is altogether an unforgettable experience to

divest oneself of ruthless materialism and truly live for a while. But even so, as the Master points out, you take the same mind with you, and in that atmosphere of transcendental thought and example, one's own personal eccentricities and fallibilities stand up very much to attention, to be inspected and, if possible, suitably dealt with. This is not always an agreeable experience. Indeed, it can be in many ways quite distressing. But it is extremely salutary, and, after all, this was why we had come all those thousands of miles. Long ago, Shakespeare wrote these well-known words:

> There is a tide in the affairs of men,
> Which, taken at the flood, leads on to fortune;
> Omitted, all the voyage of their life
> Is bound in shallows and in miseries.
>
> *Julius Caesar*

And now we realized that certainly our affairs were at the flood. Here at last was the Master of our search.

But how can I speak rationally of the Master? Like everyone else we were familiar with masters who teach in schools. Like theosophists and hosts of other students, we were familiar with the idea of Masters in the sense of perfected men, but to us they were vague astral or transcendental ideals whom one never saw nor met and who were said to meet together at full moon, deep in the Himalaya mountains. But here, in Beas, was a Master of the transcendental: not merely a teacher, but a realized soul, a perfect Adept, a Satguru, a saint with a vital spiritual technique for all and with awe-inspiring wisdom and conduct.

The traditional Christian concept of a canonized saint differs from the sainthood referred to in Sant

Mat. He or she is one who led a markedly saintly life, who performed miracles or at whose grave or habitat miraculous phenomena have occurred. Both in the East and West such terms as saint and holy man are freely and loosely used. But in the Sant Mat context, a saint or Satguru is one whose consciousness is equally at home throughout the several great regions of the universe, from matter to spirit up to Sach Khand (the true heaven and our original home). He is free to come and go at will throughout these regions.

A Sant Mat saint may be a teacher who lovingly initiates disciples and trains them to turn inwards. Thenceforth, he never leaves them. He is with them throughout life, at the time of death and on the long spiritual journey through those same regions that he knows so well.

It would be foolish of me to attempt here any description of such a one as the Master at Beas. To his disciples it would be entirely inadequate, and to others it would seem to be over-fulsome or even extravagantly imaginative.

His house is simple but is furnished tastefully throughout and is redolent with spiritual delight. His garden likewise is aromatic with jasmine, orange and rose, with a deep all-pervading tranquillity—this notwithstanding the constant coming and going of seekers and disciples and the special occasions that are generously frequent. The gateway of the garden when we were there was presided over by a most saintly sadhu with purest white beard and turban.

The satsangs or discourses were naturally in the local tongue, Punjabi, and non-Indian devotees, whose numbers were small at the time, were usually invited to the Master's house in the evening to be instructed in English. So many unusual things happen in and around Maharaj Ji's residence. One small but very recurrent thing, for instance: almost everyone we knew had many, many questions to ask, but rarely were they put because they all seemed to fade away, and the answers became self-apparent even perhaps while walking to his house. This feeling of inner communication with the Master seemed to be so natural as to scarcely raise comment except from a newcomer.

There is always a mass of work (seva) to be done in and around the colony, which is rapidly developing and enlarging its amenities, and the satsangis—visitors and residents alike—voluntarily band together by the thousands to do it, no matter what its nature. The results are truly astonishing. In the recovery of this one-time jungle land along the river banks, which have been torn into small ravines by flooding river torrents, hills are literally moved by hand and the crevasses filled up with them—not by modern expensive engineering, but by the basketful. Soil, bricks, anything can be seen being transported in these baskets upon the heads of thousands of devoted followers in endless, ant-like movement. This seva is treated by them, who may include all ranks of society and castes and some Western followers, as a spontaneous, loving and enjoyable offering to the Satguru. It is a physically dirty but spiritually cleansing experience in humility.

Maharaj Ji invariably goes to scan these activities, and the smiling faces light up even more with joy as he approaches. It is indeed a light-hearted operation from beginning to end, and one is staggered by what he observes. Indeed, the quality of all-pervading love is the keynote of the teachings of the saints, and the Master himself, as might be expected, is an outstanding example of love. He radiates it at all times. Those in his vicinity are keenly aware of it. Those in far distant places are also kept aware of it in stressful times, such as illness, accidents and even death, as well as in meditation.

Almost every satsangi has some heartwarming and dramatic story to tell of the Master's grace. The recounting of miracles, however, is not encouraged in Sant Mat, for the teaching is that true faith must be founded upon personal, inner experience, upon a deep and lasting love for the Lord and not upon proof by phenomena and miracles. One can be so easily misled by these things, which are not in themselves the hallmark of a saint. Many yogis can perform miraculous things, and many yogis are not saints.

The wisdom of this caution can be clearly seen after a little study of Sant Mat. Nevertheless, there are countless authentic and wonderful stories of the Master's instant help in times of grave difficulty—as in the Quetta earthquake, as in the dreadful days of the partition of India, when many thousands of lives were saved, and even as in our own small personal circles, at home and abroad. Indeed, one of the delights of the "social" life in the colony is listening to stories of love and devotion to the Master and of his reciprocal grace, many of which have been enacted before one's own eyes. One such incident experienced personally by the author is related as the epilogue to this book.

At Christmas time the Master, who respects all religions, invited his Western guests to a simple but delightful lunch in his own house. The Master never interferes with or disparages the religious tenets of newcomers or seekers, for these tenets have helped and nurtured their faith so far. Rather, he seeks to show them the deeper truths of their own upbringing. He will, however, often rescue and enlighten a soul that, like a pot-bound plant, is urgently seeking room to expand and grow to fulfilment. The pot-bound soul is often stifled by too much intellectualism, rituals and theology, be it Christian, Muslim, Buddhist or any other denomination. But Sant Mat, the teaching of all true saints, will enlighten the inner meaning of all creeds and is the way of fulfilment of all creeds.

A seeker will then see why the statement is sometimes made that all religions are the same. They are not, of course—far from it. One can see in the teachings of the great saints of all ages their universal and lofty purport. But after their passing, their various loving (or warring) followers start religious sects to perpetuate their own interpretation of a saint's teaching. But of the purpose of the saints themselves, Maharaj Charan Singh says:

> Saints are Men of God, who come here on a mission of mercy, to lead suffering humanity back to the feet of God. That is their only mission in life.
>
> The source of peace is in you yourself, but there must be someone to guide you to it, and for that a living Master is needed. The treasure is buried within you and you must have a chart and a guide in order to dig it out and utilize it for yourself. It is kept for you and is always there but that unerring Power sees to it that you get it only when you can properly utilize it.
>
> *Light on Sant Mat*

3

THE ETERNAL QUEST

It would be presumptuous for the author of this book to infer that meeting with the Sant Mat philosophy is an experience that will create a radical change in one's outlook and sentiment, for it depends upon whether or not one is ready for such a change. There are many who do not feel the call to pursue any particular metaphysical or spiritual study. They only wish to dally pleasurably on the way.

It is one thing to live a life from day to day, experiencing a few transient joys and a lot of punishment, in other words, living a comparatively ordinary, humdrum, reasonably moral life. It is quite another thing to find oneself reaching out for the very heart of life. Sometimes this momentous thing happens to a very fortunate person overnight, but to most of us, it comes rather slowly and in stages.

I know of followers of Sant Mat who have walked into it, so to speak, as if walking into their own home. There are others like myself, with a good Christian background, who have traced a long but fascinating journey, step by step, along a comparatively well-worn philosophic road—a road dotted with "isms," "osophies," and "ologies," all hospitable oases—and each step has furthered the desire to take the next in the direction of that tremendous but unknown 'something' towards which every aspirant feels he must hasten.

In schooldays, one goes from class to class and from school to school. Unless one is foolish, he does not reject or belittle the teaching of each, but builds upon them, retaining grateful memories of the teachers. It would be presumptuous to say that any one religion or system of philosophy is either right or wrong. They all serve their purpose, just as our schools cover, in their own time and place, that long journey from infancy to young adulthood. Similarly one feels thankful for having contacted so many schools of thought, so many teachers, so many angles of approach leading up to Sant Mat—thankful to one group for its presentation of reincarnation, to another for its exposition of the working principles of matter, to still another for its demonstration of karmic laws and physical limitations.

For my wife and I, the several great world religions created a conflict in our minds because of their rigid adherence to narrow rituals and opposing dogmas. Upon contact with Sant Mat, some peace of reconciliation descended, for such is the transcendental, unifying power of this great and holy teaching and its practice. We began to see through so many misinterpretations and to coordinate basic truths.

Without ritual, without churches, without mosques or temples, Sant Mat is the very core and spirit of esoteric study and practice, especially the latter. It tears through the veil—or, rather, it quietly dissolves the many films of dirt that obscure the spiritual scene and obstruct the one-time natural vision that was, and still is, the heritage of spiritual man.

On adopting the Sant Mat philosophy, the problems of life become more manageable, for they are put on a personal level. Sant Mat holds that one must concentrate on his own salvation before attempting to help the rest of the world, because no one can give to others something he does not possess himself. This *individual* redemption is the core of the original teaching of the great saints of all ages, and it is regarded as the great ideal, the eternal truth.

But, strangely enough, there seems to be a marked criticism of those who wish to lead a more serene or less sophisticated life: Privacy, seclusion, retreat, meditation—these are strange words in this hectic age. And are they not often interpreted as escapism or pure selfishness? How often is that impatient and misguided question heard: why not do something useful?

But it must be very clear that a meditative life does not preclude good action; rather it enhances discretion. It is this very indulgence in activities that often masquerade as useful that has contracted our heavy burden of sin, or karma, for these activities are as often as not motivated by pure materialism, fatuity or egotism. It requires much discrimination literally to mind one's own business and to avoid incurring heavy debts of karma.

The world is a battlefield where creatures are constantly at war with one another. Even lifeless elements—water and earth, acid and alkali—are locked in a continuous struggle. It has always been so in spite of what man considers progress—higher standards of living, scientific discoveries and so on. At first glance it would seem, then, that against this irresistible Amazonian current of behaviour in the world of Mammon or Caesar, the individual is helpless. But the individual is not helpless, and the situation is by no means hopeless. We are again and again being reminded of that.

But just what can one aspiring individual do? Certainly he cannot do that which all the giants could not do—he cannot change the world or its behaviour. Indeed, it is far from expedient to try, for as the Franco-Swiss philosopher Alphonse Karr once said, "The more things change, the more they remain the same." Is it not striking that some four thousand years ago news headlines in the bazars might have read: "All Traffic in Red Sea Held up by Trouble Between Israelites and Egyptians," or "Urgent Investigation into Gross Sex Perversion—Sodom and Gomorrah to be Purged." Headlines of today merely have different place names.

Man cannot alter the laws of the world, but he can alter his attitude and relationship to it. Physical evolution is a painfully slow business, and moral growth is scarcely less so. Our animal passions are still as strong and as besetting, but spiritual enlightenment of individual souls is another matter entirely. In the savagery of human history there have always been outstanding examples of humanitarianism, such as King Ashoka of India and, of course, all the Messiahs. But never were the lower layers of animalism more apparent than today.

As far as man is concerned, Shakespeare says, "All the world's a stage," where the human puppet, imprisoned by his own karmas, acts the little part in which he is cast and goes through the motions of living and dying, waking and sleeping. Yet man in his inner being is always subtly aware that that is decidedly not all. There is behind the play of life an unquenchable yearning, the groping of one who has eyes but sees not and ears but hears not.

Possibly the most frequent question that man breathes to the silent air is the one so full of pathos and longing: what is it all about? It is too profound and persistent a question to be ignored. Unfortunately, those specialists who might give one an answer—specialists in theology and ritual, in sociology, in science, in psychology, in economics—are so rarely in agreement that one's confusion is compounded. This often leads to what is called disillusionment but is more likely to be egotistic frustration and damaged pride. True disillusionment should be a thing of joy—a state of being rid of mirages, illusions, unwarranted fears and fantasies and of being ready to accept some wider experience of truth.

The only hope of peace and sweet reasonableness is in the practice of simplicity and humility, which leads to a very different set of values. These are the qualities, above all else, that are both exhibited and expected by the sages who have achieved serenity, by Masters and mystics of all times who have endeavoured to give the answer to those with the ears to hear. These mystics tell us that humility is the armour of the saints and their devotees.

Unfortunately for us the mind is greatly averse to these qualities of simplicity and humility. The mind, which admires scholarship and has such wonderful achievements to its credit, glories also in tortuous byplay, in self-adulation, in intrigue, in conventions, rules and regulations, in splitting hairs and in clever interpretations. It is itself the almost insuperable barrier to those lofty states of spiritual devotion, gnosis (inner knowledge) and consciousness far transcending the mental—to states that do not conform to the realms of logic or physics, yet are infinitely more real and reliable.

It should be humbling to us to realize our real position in the creation. Consider the story of the little boy who was infinitely fascinated by the sight of aeroplanes leaving the ground and disappearing into the horizon. His mother promised that he, too, would be given a flight one day. When it came about and they were airborne, he sat for a while entranced with wonderment, but he finally risked a whisper to his mother: "Mummy, when do we begin to get small?" The little voyager did not realize that he had already become smaller than a pin point from the perspective of those at the airport. Nor did he realize that the people at the airport had diminished also to the point where he could no longer see them.

From a larger perspective, the aeroplane, the boy, the airport and his mother were all points on or around the earth. And the earth itself is but a tiny speck in the heavens. The geometrician describes a point as a position in space with no magnitude. It is easy, therefore, to see that even in the physical universe we individuals have no magnitude. What, then, can we say of the universe unknown to ordinary men that separates man from God? Of our perceptions to the contrary, the mystic would say that such thoughts are just tricks of the mind that one would expect. But if the mind, which is so powerful, can be trained and enlisted in the work of self-realization, then it becomes a true ally and a messenger of the gods.

Ancient mythology was possibly more wisely informed on this matter than we realize. For instance, in the Roman spiritual hierarchy, mind is represented by Mercury, the winged messenger of the gods—a demi-god, a servant attendant upon his master. But today the mind is more than inclined to abuse its privileges and usurp the power of its master, the soul because the contemporary worship of science places mind upon the supreme throne of the universe. This is at variance with the endless exhortations of saints and sages, who warn us that wordly pleasures and achievements are both transitory and very dearly bought. We have to go much deeper for reality.

With all the glories and fascinations of our age of scientific inquiry, there is still that same background of longing and wonder: what is it all about? And those in tribulation may also wonder: why should it happen to me? The seeker who is not convinced by the answers of sectarian theologies of East or West must of necessity leave those groups and promote his own search for the master guide who will take him along the straight and narrow pathway back to the Father's home—back to his own scarcely remembered home.

It is in a way a lonely journey, for he cannot take the world with him. It is obviously a long difficult journey—no saint or messiah has declared it otherwise—but it has its own supreme joys. The journey, once started, requires much thought, discipline and above all meditation of a particular kind.

It is incumbent upon the seeker to try to find the

teacher, the discipline and the way which best fit his capabilities, as his awareness develops and his values change. The Sant Mat Master not only personally instructs, he also gives one a map of the inner geography, so to speak, and a description of the regions to be traversed. And he is the unfailing friend and companion throughout the journey.

4

EXPANDING CONSCIOUSNESS

If one were to try to find the best possible example of a paradox in the whole world, he would conclude that life itself, as humans live it, is the greatest. For instance, we say that the best things in life are free but we spend our years religiously in pursuit of money to buy high-priced material comforts. Some pessimist has said gloomily that in the midst of life we are in death, yet we do little about it, remaining wrapped up in our little make-beliefs and false perceptions.

In the welter of paradoxes that is our daily portion, we are so dependent on snatching at anything that looks fortunate, or seems to be a lucky gamble, that a great difficulty presents itself to layman and cleric alike. It is the difficulty of finding, and then of holding the true conviction that there really is an expanded consciousness in which luck and ill-fortune have no place; that there *is* something that belongs not only to the hereafter, but to the here and now; something for everyday use that is made of gold but is not dearly bought; something that fulfils the perpetual longing for spiritual enlightenment; something that gives authentic answers through experience. This consciousness can be experienced individually, and it is a rich treasure that can and does compensate completely for the so-called sacrifice of a few of our dearly bought but very transient, pleasures.

There are many opinions as to what constitutes a spiritual way of life. Some sets of standards would be considered merely ethics and quite elementary, while some would seem so lofty as to be attainable only by uniquely privileged and saintly souls, such as those honoured in the holy books of the various religions. For some, even for many deep thinkers, a moral and ethical life of humanitarianism is sufficient; but to others, that is but a necessary clearing of the site to prepare for spiritual building and for deeper transcendental experiences. Surrounded as they are by the paradoxes of their familiar way of life, their attention is called sooner or later to the philosophy of the wise men of the East, the middle way, a most desirable but at the same time a most difficult one to follow.

> Saints and Masters wish to take all souls out of the labyrinth of this coarse material plane, but the masses are always searching for happiness in the gratification of the debasing appetites of the senses. Little do they dream of the bliss and the beauty of higher worlds, to which man can rise in this very life.
>
> When the Saints reveal this fact, most people look upon them with suspicion. They do not trust them, for the orthodox religions have long since forgotten about the existence of the Divine Music of the Word, and the masses of mankind still tend to believe that:
>
> "Sweet is this life alone;
> The next, to none is known."
>
> *Discourses on Sant Mat,*
> Maharaj Sawan Singh

The saints teach that there are two paths to

choose from: one being the path of scholarly knowledge (*gyan*), the other, that of devotion (*bhakti*). The first, that of academic knowledge and rectitude, though very impressive and attractive, is exoteric and belongs to the world of mind, matter and formality. The second, that of devotion, belongs to the soul and is esoteric. The path of knowledge, we are told, is of the brain or intellect and will pass away at the time of death. The path of devotion, however, is of the soul, which is eternal, and it transcends the hazards both of the material world and of death and rebirth.

It is this latter path—of devotion, of meditation and of contemplation—that leads to the higher states of expanded consciousness referred to by all the saints and mystics. These states are not the prerogative of the favoured few but are the attainable heritage of that long-suffering creature called Everyman, should he so desire it. But that desire is crucial. As stated before, the Master points out that one must choose between two basic attitudes, that of the worldly man (*manmukh*) and that of the devotee (*gurmukh*). The worldly man has his heart in created things, while the devotee has his heart in the Creator Himself.

When Bulleh Shah, a Mohammedan mystic, writes:

> When I learned the lesson of love
> My mind rebelled against church and mosque.
> I entered the real Temple of the Lord (the body)
> Where a thousand instruments played.
> I found my Beloved in my house.

Or when a songwriter pens the line, "Mine eyes have seen the glory of the coming of the Lord," they obviously do not mean that they have heard a musical rendering or seen a beautiful sunset or wonderful flowers blooming. They are speaking figuratively of an expansion of consciousness beyond the realm of physical dimensions. Equally obviously, these experiences are not confined to race or creed or era.

There is a very simple but apt story told by Maharaj Sawan Singh:

> A beautiful white swan, whose home was the sea, was once flying from one ocean to another. Feeling tired, he descended to the earth and rested on the edge of a well. A frog from inside the well hopped up to him and asked who he was. He replied that he was a poor swan from the sea. The frog then enquired how big the sea was, and the swan replied that it was vast in area. The frog retreated a few hops and asked if he had covered as much area as the sea. The swan, greatly amused, told him that the sea was much bigger than that. The frog then hopped a much larger distance and asked if he had not correctly measured the area of the ocean. The swan of course said no. Desperately the frog jumped around the entire curve of the well and asked if that indeed gave an exact estimate of the vastness of the sea. The swan again replied that it did not. Thereupon, the frog called him a liar and a knave, for the sea could never have a bigger area than the world in which he (the frog) was living.
>
> *Discourses on Sant Mat*

Like the frog, we have no way of proving the validity of the experiences of others except by duplicating them ourselves. Those who have not yet experienced expanded consciousness or felt it desirable to adopt the method of inner discipline needed to develop this consciousness might perhaps still agree to this simple analogy: until we have learned the alphabet, we have no conception of the joys and advancement denied to us by our illiteracy. We cannot even guess the extent of the new horizons that would open up if we would discipline ourselves to learn those simple ABC's.

A child may at first be reluctant to apply himself to the task of learning the alphabet, but he does not yet know, except by hearsay, that such acquisition is the key that will open up for him the vast field of literature. At that stage of his evolution, the possibility means little to him. By the same token, techniques of proper meditation are the spiritual ABC's. As Maharaj Ji puts it, "the acquisition of the secret of Nam" is the key to the vaster field of spiritual and metaphysical experience wherein lies the truth of that sublime directive—the kingdom of heaven is within; seek it there.

It is significant that the first of the paths before us, scholarly knowledge, requires the care and instruction of a living master together with the diligent application of the pupil. This we accept without question! But the second path, that of devotion, calls even more for the closest relationship between a true Master and his pupil. This relationship in its highest form persists into the sublime states, far beyond the bounds of death, that are so well known to true saints and mystics. It eventually severs the bonds of karma that keep us bound to the wheel of births and deaths (reincarnation). Without the wisdom and help of the true Master, that cannot be accomplished.

It is this salvation from earthly bondage that is at the core of the teachings of all the great saints. It is for this purpose that the saints have come into this world, not once, not twice, but at all times and in all ages, and they continue to do so. The age-old teaching is given out again and again, in the idiom of the time, with a rejuvenating freshness that clears away the ancient cobwebs.

The present century is certainly not without its pure wells of spiritual teaching. The almost startling simplicity of the eternal verities is again presented in Sant Mat. It would be difficult to find a way of life and a system of spiritual training more practical, more enlightened, more comprehensive or, indeed, more suitable to the twentieth century.

However, even under the immediate supervision and example of such a great and living saint as the Master at Beas, the stumbling efforts of the disciple do not so readily change into accomplishments that one can sit back and let things happen. The disciple is charged with the task of raising his attention, by correct meditation, to the point of consciousness in the forehead behind the eyes. This constitutes the first true spiritual step, and it must become a daily practice, for it is the starting point of all true mystical experience. "I will lift up mine eyes unto the Lord." In other words, I will deliberately raise my attention to the point of greater consciousness and of true values.

This point of consciousness, known by so many names—the eye of the needle, the wicket gate, *tisra til*, the third eye, the tenth door—is the great threshold or starting point of the inward journey. It is referred to again and again in scriptures as going to the mountain top or to a high place. Above this point lies Tao, the Way, the road to new values and relationships in a world of joy and happiness, while below it lies the world of sorrow. Above it is the transcendental, the road to Sach Khand,[1] below it is the material world of Mammon, our attachment to which keeps us on the treadmill of karma and reincarnation.

It would be well to note here that this practice of concentration has nothing whatsoever to do with inducing trances or mediumistic states; rather it is an exercise designed to give one greatly increased awareness and clear vision. It is not a matter of thinking, it is a question of making the mind clear and still, with the attention focused at the crucial point of consciousness, the transcendental eye. The concentration to be achieved is a state as delicate as that of a jeweller's balance come to rest gently in mid-air upon its fulcrum. It causes no strain on the eyes, no frown on the forehead; it brings instead a state of great peace.

How to reach this point and to sustain it, to make the transcendental moment last, to carry its effects into all ills and troubles of life and through death? By the instruction of the Master and the diligence of the pupil. The Master at initiation awakens the pupil to the highest qualities that lie latent within him.

The present Master, Maharaj Charan Singh, writes to a disciple:

> What you say is true. The world is full of misery, selfishness, cruelty and greed. Your Master [Maharaj Sawan Singh] used to say, and all the other Saints say so too, that if you want to find happiness and peace in this world, or anywhere below the two eyes, you will not succeed. In the same way, it would be equally impossible to find misery and cruelty above the eye center.

---

[1]The highest heaven, beyond Par Brahm.

> It is true that karmas play a great part, and all this drama is staged by our own karmas. The only way to get out of it and to find peace is to withdraw yourself, by concentration at the eye center, repeating the five Holy Names with faith and devotion, and attaining shelter and peace in the Sound Current.
>
> *Light on Sant Mat*

Surely these words are of the utmost significance to all seekers of enlightenment. It would be difficult to come across a fundamental truth so simply and so clearly put as this.

5

PARADOX AND JIGSAW PUZZLE

If a real sense of urgency ever comes, to investigate personally this more stable life of inner contemplation and to take part in the happier states of existence beyond the material world, it will be necessary to take stock of one's present life. Within living memory, there can be few people in the world whose lives have not been so fragmented by wars, revolutions and economic upheavals that they do not appear to be chaotic. It is difficult, then, not to regard our passing years as a jumble of haphazard incidents interspersed with good or ill luck. These incidents seem as disconnected as an unthreaded pile of rough beads.

Life, as such, is indeed incomprehensible. But it is encouraging to think that a jigsaw puzzle, which our lives resemble, also begins as a tangled mass of pieces. When these pieces are carefully reassembled, they disclose a completely unsuspected beauty.

There are many qualities that help in putting odd pieces together so that they make sense. They are the same qualities required, for instance, by the archaeologist, a supreme collector of bits and pieces, out of which he builds the fascinating pictures of history. The same skill is also shown by the detective, who collects evidence and despises no clue, however tenuous, to track down the truth. These qualities include confidence, determination, faith, patience in trial and error, a quick sense for the minutest intuitive hints and, above all, an open mind. All these are also required to review one's life, if it is to be seen in its correct perspective and, like a completed jigsaw puzzle, as a coherent whole, a picture created by "Him who knew what He was doing." One then realizes that the puzzling aspects of life are caused by our incomplete glimpses of it and that a true and comprehensive picture can be obtained by using the proper technique.

Suppose one considers, for a moment, the enormous industry built on violence, brutality and crime. One may be outraged at the debasing sordidness of books, plays and films whose plots turn on mayhem and terror, but if one protests, he is usually told that life is like that, and it is necessary to portray reality.

Here is where the philosophy of Sant Mat raises a powerful challenge. Is life really like that sordid, dead-end rat race, or have we overlooked something? And even if life is thought to be like that, can it be useful to feed upon macabre subjects for entertainment? Does it elevate the mind? Does it raise the consciousness? Does it help the situation? Why look for reality through lust, fear, violence and a dead body? Why not start with a living body, your own for instance? If one begins to see his own story in this way, he will not then be chasing fiction but discovering truth. Indeed, one can even aspire to solve the greatest mystery of all.

One cannot be too often reminded that self-consciousness comes before God-consciousness. It is necessary first to have the desire to reach a deeper understanding of the facts of life, then to collect all one's resources and talents and then to coordinate them with a sense of purpose.

It is ironic that so many people insist, perhaps out of modesty, more often out of dejection, that they know so little when, in fact, everyone possesses a vast amount of knowledge, infinitely more than they are aware of. Maybe they are not able, or do not care, to coordinate their own chaotic, uncharted knowledge. But tucked away inside them is all the knowledge of the conscious, the subconscious and the superconscious worlds that they have gleaned from many, many lives. It is there to draw upon, more or less at will, if the will is there and the way is followed.

The Masters have said that one of the most urgent things in this world is self-discovery. Who is the self? In pursuit of an answer, one must ask, with great sincerity, "How did I arrive at my present circumstances? Was it accidental? Was it luck, or was it somehow in the divine scheme?" And one must try to answer with the truth, the whole truth and nothing but the truth.

These are the most serious and profound questions man may ever put to himself, and to pursue their answers with an open mind requires some quiet courage. It also requires much faith and a great deal of hope, for someone who reviews his own life may find that he is looking at a person in peculiar, and perhaps far from straightforward, circumstances—a victim of "the slings and arrows of outrageous fortune." Faith and hope are needed to reassure the searcher that although the person he sees is himself, it is not his true self.

This is one of the many paradoxes that will confront one who pursues the path of self-realization. But it is reasonable to say that he who discovers a paradox is on the verge of knowing truth. The head and tail of a penny are diametrically opposed, but its value is represented by both sides together. Parallel lines may never meet, but they form the rails on which a train may reach its station.

In the exacting task of self-investigation, we must steadfastly retain an open mind, not caring in the least if some favourite preconceived ideas have to be modified or even reversed. Nothing in our lives is too irrelevant to examine, nothing too small. We may see time and time again that two ideas, two revered ideologies, two conventions, two pieces of the same puzzle, do not fit comfortably together in spite of some similarity. Turn them around, place them differently, and they slide home with ease. So too will many of our incompatibles.

In the end, one will probably be surprised to find himself becoming something of a philosopher and mystic, the richest of men. This would be a very great step, for it is undoubtedly the way to peace and harmony. The study of the self might also lead to what Christianity calls salvation because, as the saints have said, when the *chela* (pupil) is ready, the guru (Master) appears. This meeting is neither coincidental nor accidental, but it may occur in strange and indirect ways, as borne out by the following accounts.

A Canadian officer attached to the international military force somewhere in Viet Nam was instructed in the course of duty to meet another officer at the railway station there. This he did and noticed that the newcomer, a Sikh, was carrying a book under his arm. Being interested in books, the Canadian inquired as to its name and origin and was told that it was, strangely enough, an American book on Eastern subjects, namely, *The Path of the Masters*, by Dr. Julian Johnson, one of the first books on Sant Mat in English. The Canadian, a captain, was offered the loan of it.

For him it happened to be the transcendental moment, because the contents were the answer to his longings. He immediately dispatched a cable to the Master at Beas, requesting an audience. Thereupon, as so often happens in Sant Mat, many unlikely things fell naturally into place. The captain obtained ten days' leave and took a plane from Saigon to Delhi, where the Master was at that time. The plane was late, but Maharaj Ji, in his solicitude, stayed up until 1 a.m. to greet the newcomer. They then took the train northwards to Beas where, during a five day stay, the captain was instructed in the philosophy of Sant Mat before returning to his more worldly problems, but also to a completely altered life.

Another story also concerns a military officer, a colonel. One of his juniors was in trouble, and the case had been brought to him for disposal. All the circumstantial evidence was against the accused, who nevertheless firmly proclaimed his innocence. In his sworn testimony he indicated that it was virtually impossible for him to behave in the way alleged since his whole philosophy of life was contrary to it.

The colonel felt impelled to investigate the truth of such a strange defence and visited the source of the philosophy given by the prisoner. It was, as the reader can imagine, Beas, and the compelling philosophy was the teachings of the Saints. The charges proved to be baseless, and the colonel had also found his beloved Satguru.

A third story comes to mind of two brothers who were in search of inner knowledge. They were in a business together with two branches, one brother being in northern India and the other considerably to the south. The southern one (and elder) had spent much of his time for some years in the practice of yogas. He tried austerities, fasting and physical discipline requiring incredible endurance, with no results except extreme ill-health. This led finally to a wholesale rejection of all spiritual or mystical interests, and a life of complete extroversion.

His brother meanwhile had met the Master. During a visit to Beas, he hopefully asked his elder brother to come and investigate Sant Mat, which he was sure would prove fruitful. The answer was an indignant refusal and an order for him to come south at once to attend to business.

But the younger brother persisted, finally asking at least to be met at Amritsar, thirty miles distant from Beas. This was arranged, but when they met, the younger one "discovered" that he had conveniently left his baggage at Beas and must go back to retrieve it. The elder brother, although exasperated, accompanied him, and by attending satsang, made contact with the Master and the philosophy. His seemingly fruitless search was finally triumphant almost in spite of himself, for Sant Mat was exactly what he had previously sought in the wrong places.

6

VICTIM AND CULPRIT

If perchance you happen to be one of those people who is satisfied with life as you find it, then either you are a most fortunate person, or you have your eyes tightly closed, or your glasses are, for the moment, rose-tinted. If so, you will probably not agree with that great modern sage, Maharaj Sawan Singh Ji, often simply called the Great Master, when he says:

> Worldly happiness is only an illusion, for what seems to be happiness is only momentary and brings suffering in its wake.
>
> There is no happiness here, wherever we might be born. There is only misery and suffering everywhere. Just look around. In this world, who is happy? How hard is the horse whipped to make it go faster! The overworked bullock drops down fatigued and exhausted but, pierced with the goad, is forced to get up to work again. And the goats, cattle, fowl, etc., how they are mercilessly slaughtered to fill our bellies. Do we ever think how we would feel if we were to change places with them and suffer similar tortures? Let us not forget that the Law of Karma is inexorable and we will have to reap what we have sown.

That cruel suffering is blindly given and as blindly received accounts for the world's condition. The ancient law of an eye for an eye prevails, not as retribution or punishment or because of the wrath of God, but as the natural, logical, inexorable course of justice. In the long run, there is no miscarriage of justice, although the effect of an action may not occur within one life span. One who acts with cruelty must eventually receive the same treatment; thus does the law of cause and effect perpetuate suffering at an unfortunate level. It has been so since the creation began and will continue to be so.

But let us consider the provocative statement of the twentieth century poet Khalil Gibran: "The murdered is not unaccountable for his own murder..." It is a statement not to be dismissed lightly; indeed, it is a trenchant question that must be considered as part of the detective work of self-investigation. We know only too well who is the suffering victim, but we also have to decide who is the culprit.

The victim may regard himself with pity, but is he entirely guiltless of his own condition? How far has he brought it upon himself? Not only is it true that "as ye sow, so shall ye reap," but also that as you are reaping now, so you have sown in the past. There is always a cause before an effect, and there is always an effect after a cause. As Maharaj Sawan Singh says above, karma is inexorable. Our actions strike back or come to roost, and we are repaid in kind.

When one suffers pain or other extremities, it is valid to ask, "What have I done to deserve this?" But the query should not be put in protest or anger or petulance, but with the greatest humility. For events that may seem like disastrous strokes of ill luck, insufferable injustices or unaccountable bolts from the blue are seen in the light of Sant Mat philosophy to be the results of one's own past conduct.

The law of karma forces us to take responsibility for our actions, good and bad. We cannot disclaim liability when it appears to be advantageous, and we cannot insist upon something other than justice, however painful or inconvenient it may be. With this understanding, one can fit the pieces of his life's puzzle perfectly into an unfolding story.

Although it is saddening that "the whole creation groaneth and travailleth in pain," it is almost invariably in the depths of despair or pain that we sincerely call for enlightenment. Maharaj Charan Singh says:

> Yes, as we look back we can see that it is usually the difficulties in life which help to strengthen our desire for liberation and enlightenment because they enable us to realize more and more the transitory nature of this world and its contents.
>
> *Light on Sant Mat*

But just as a random page in a detective story is meaningless without the context provided by the preceding pages, so it is impossible to understand any event in our own lives by itself. The event can only be given its proper perspective by an understanding of karma and reincarnation.

In the evolutionary process of this material world, everything human, animal, vegetable and mineral has its tendencies, its momentum and its destiny—a state of becoming. We must not, therefore, look only at this transitory tick of the clock, the present moment, which is only a fleeting snapshot of one's life and which is already in the past before its existence can be realized. It is necessary to take a long look in retrospect at one's own footprints in the sands of time, the tracks that lead one to the discovery of why our present condition is the way it is.

Anyone who does this can scarcely fail to discern in his life a bias, a characteristic tendency, a proneness to a certain course of action. One can detect a thread of destiny, a finger of fate, something that takes on the atmosphere of inevitability. In other words, there is a definite continuum, the fate dictated by our past sowing.

7

FATE AND FREE WILL

There is a state of mind called fatalism that can, if one is not careful, lead to a dead end or disaster. It is so easy a trap to fall into and so difficult a one to get out of, for it promotes depression and inertia. From certain angles, fatalism is a plausible and convincing theory, but fate only partially determines life's events, and taken by itself, out of context, this belief can grossly distort one's judgement and conduct.

Its paradoxical opposite is of course free will, which is equally a one-legged affair. Many a bitter fight has been waged over fate versus free will. They are classic academic clichés that provide for endless intellectual hair-splitting and debate.

The truth is that fate and free will are the inseparable sides of the karmic coin. Our lives are governed by both, just as a car is controlled by both a brake and an accelerator. The fatalistic aspect of our lives is the inevitable working out of causes already initiated, for an arrow that is shot from the bow must reach its mark, and a debt incurred must in all justice be settled. The free will side is our deliberate aiming for the future by the choices we make.

Unfortunately, what we call our free will is so heavily conditioned by our environment and by the natural tendencies, biases, reflexes, inherent desires, and inbred physical, mental and spiritual compulsions that we bring with us into the world that we can hardly call it free any more. Looking back over one's life can hardly fail to produce many a sigh and exclamation of "If only I had done such and such," or "If only I had not done such and such." But if we claim that our will is entirely free, we must also say, "I had the choice, and I deliberately chose what I did." Nevertheless, what may have looked like an open opportunity was really one for which we stacked the cards or loaded the dice long ago. Our alternatives are as limited as they are for the woman who says in vain, "Ah, if only I had been a man I would have done such and such"; or for the poor person who says, "If only I'd had the money"; or for the alcoholic who says, "If only I had not been so drunk"; or for the invalid who says, "If only I had not been so ill all the time."

But everything flows from what went before, from our previous choices and acts, whether deliberate or thoughtless. Therefore, the will at any time is far from free. The stage is set for any act whatsoever. Present actions are dictated and conditioned by our own previous actions and reactions, and our fate is intertwined with the fate of others. The person who exclaims "I am the master of my fate; I am the captain of my soul" strikes a brave posture, but whatever may be his egotistic views, should he not beware of riding in a car, boarding a train or travelling by ship or plane? His life, along with the lives of his fellow passengers, is surely in the hands of the driver or the pilot. The karmas of all have brought them together to share whatsoever may occur in transit.

Since our present life is heavily conditioned and

largely determined by all our previous actions and reactions, what particularly concerns us now is that whatever responsibilities we have incurred must be discharged. Somewhere and somehow the debts must be repaid. The debits and credits that are assigned to us at birth out of the accumulation from all our past lives are called pralabdh karmas. This is our unalterable fate, often called our stars.

Shakespeare's Julius Caesar says, "The fault, dear Brutus, is not in our stars, but in ourselves, that we are underlings." For our so-called stars are of our own making. They are a statement of our assets and liabilities and as such cannot be side-stepped. They represent, in the Christian phraseology, the state to which God has been pleased to call us in this life.

A farmer cannot repudiate that which he has been sowing. Likewise, it is our inescapable fate to harvest what we have sown, however misguided the sowing. How we glory in those harvests when they are good, and how we complain when they are poor.

Having realized the true relationship between our present actions and our future destiny, there looms the problem of what to do about it—what steps to take to use our modicum of free will to the best possible advantage. The answer is—to find a Master who can free us from the endless cycles of karma. He should be one who does not point the way that we must go but beckons from ahead. In other words, he must himself be a Master of the way. Our task then is to work with him.

> Sant Mat is the practical part of self-realization, and Shabd or the inner Sound Current is the essential part of Sant Mat... One is put into contact

> with this Sound Current by a Master—a realized soul—who is himself well versed in it.
>
> Maharaj Sawan Singh

Whether or not we find a Master is also part of our destiny, but if we respond to that inner pull for happiness of a higher order and begin the search, we are sowing seeds that will sooner or later be ripe for harvest. And from where does that inner pull come? Here again Shakespeare's words are apt:

> There's a divinity that shapes our ends,
> Rough-hew them how we will.

And thank God that is the way of it; our final destiny is in other and wiser hands.

8

GOD CANNOT REVEAL HIMSELF TO THE CONTAMINATED MIND

Man washes his body with water, but in his heart there is evil of every description.

Ravi Das

It has always been the natural habit of playwrights, authors, journalists and broadcasters to dramatize life. However, to dramatize it is not necessarily to tell the truth about it, but rather to exaggerate one side of it, to caricature it by understatement or overstatement. And what is it that makes for popular drama? Stark tragedy—the starker the better—coupled with sex and psychological distortions presented with passionate force. With few exceptions, it is the rule to exploit, to stir up and to advertise the emotional upheavals of man at his grossest level. Take, as an example, this quotation from a daily newspaper: "The dark and secret passions and prejudices, which lurk never far below the surface of daily life, have come bursting through."

Moralists aver that crime does not pay. Many authors and playwrights may also pay lip service to this principle, professing to be demonstrating it in their novels and plays portraying the relationships between man and man and between man and woman at their lowest and most depraved level. One is tempted to wonder if these self-avowed moralists wish to help cure the evils they juggle with so cleverly or merely to exist like leeches upon them. Because they are, in fact, capitalizing on man's lowest tendencies, drawing fabulous royalties from their writings, unaware what devastating seeds of karma they are sowing for themselves by contaminating the minds of their audience.

It is a maxim in journalistic and entertainment circles that uplift rarely pays; it has no box office appeal! Perhaps it does not pay in royalties deposited in the bank account or in profits to the publisher, but the kind of drama that is financially profitable exacts more payment than it gives. We know it is possible to clean a stable with a stream of clear water, but it does not help simply to stir it up with a stick or throw more dung into it; the one who does the stirring only becomes more soiled. This helps to explain why many authors, playwrights and actors who deal in low drama have themselves to seek the psychiatrist's couch or tranquillizing drugs.

The price paid by these same authors and playwrights is compounded by karmic responsibility. The pen is mightier than the sword; therefore, it can be more destructive. These writers and their producers have the responsibility for the effect of their works on the many who read or see them.

One of the teachings of the Masters is very much to the point here. Even the most casual student of psychology knows that a bad habit or indulgence is not made better by fanning it, by feeding it or by dwelling on it. It is only cured by replacing it with something more interesting, more attractive and more arresting to the mind. And the saints point out that, since the world began its debasement of spiritual, mental and physical currency, there have also been sages and messiahs who have patiently taught to those in the mood or in the condition to listen that untold joy and riches exist within, far surpassing those without.

But this is much too simple and naïve to appeal to the senses or to the "rational" mind until the stress of life has brought us to the verge of nausea and exhaustion, until the battered body, the humiliated mind and the weary soul cry out "How long, O Lord, how long?" And if we need drama, what could be more dramatic than the gentle answer, "Be still, and learn that I, within you, am God and Peace."

As the Master says, God cannot reveal Himself to the contaminated mind. So it is away from worldly entertainments that the technique of self- and God-consciousness is to be practised—in the silence and harmony of the unstruck music, the heavenly Word or Bani. This is the underlying and absolutely essential message of the great spiritual teachers the world over.

Indeed, all true religious teachings and philosophies have this and so many other things in common that one wonders at the seemingly insuperable divergencies. Perhaps it is helpful to remember that probably just as many Christians do not realize the truths of other religions—such as Buddhism, Hinduism, Islam, Sikhism, and Taoism—as the followers of these have not heard the truths and aims of basic Christianity. Generally speaking, the followers of each are painfully ignorant of what the other philosophies stand for. We are at a great disadvantage in our spiritual search without a wider appreciation of them.

Even an arm-chair survey of the various great religions, such as one may find in *The Path of the Masters*, by Julian Johnson, will demonstrate the extraordinary number of similarities underlying the diversity of dogmas. After this short examination, one can be assured that the prime source and object is the same for all, there being but one God or Beloved or Absolute, as they all state. The divergencies and discrepancies can only be due to human elements that invariably seem to confuse and obscure the objective.

Again and again the similarities of sentiment in these religions are so obvious that when one reads a passage without knowing its source, he often wonders from which holy book it was taken. This is true of the following:

> What is the good of running to the forest to find the Lord? He resides within you and pervades all your being, yet is apart. God is within you as the perfume is in the flower and the image in the mirror. He is deep down at the bottom of your hearts. There He must be sought.
>
> Guru Nanak

> The kingdom of God is within you.
>
> New Testament

> We should see God with our inner eye and hear His voice with our inner ear. We should penetrate the dark veil within and behold His glory.
>
> Shams-i-Tabriz

> O man, listen to the sublime teaching of the saints. They give out what they have seen with their own eyes.
>
> Guru Nanak

> Be still, and know that I am God.
>
> Old Testament

The words 'still' and 'within' are common to all higher philosophies and are of great significance, because they are also used by the great modern saints of Beas in teaching their method of meditation. The need for stillness can be illustrated by a simple analogy with scientific research. Anyone who has used a microscope or a telescope will appreciate at once that the reason for using it is to augment the normal power of the physical eyes to explore fields not normally seen and usually very little known.

To achieve this objective, the following steps must be taken:

1. Place the instrument upon a firm and reliable base.
2. Make sure that the lenses are clean.
3. Bring the subject matter within reasonable range.
4. Avoid interruptions, dismiss all distractions of the mind and calm the emotions.
5. Remove all prejudices and preconceived ideas; keep the mind receptive.
6. Operate the fine focus with a delicate touch until motion becomes nil, after which action gives way to contemplation.

Those who have worked with a microscope know that there is a somewhat trying period of adjusting the focus, during which nothing sharp appears. Then something comes for a flash that may be lost and retrieved again and again until it is finally retained. Then the object of study is revealed to the watcher, who will contemplate and evaluate what he sees. Such revelations have often had a very great influence on the physical world.

To experience revelations that will have a similar influence on our spiritual lives, we must focus our minds until we achieve the stillness of contemplation. Have you ever seriously tried to be still in order to attain sharp, accurate vision? Not just to sit still for a moment, but to be still through and through. To experience stillness in the sense inferred by the commands "Be still, and know," "Watch and pray" or "He that hath ears to hear, let him hear." To be still to the profound depths needed to listen to the voice of silence, or to the heavenly Bani of Guru Nanak, or to the unspoken language or unstruck music of Maharaj Sawan Singh. To be still enough to experience the "peace. . .which passeth all understanding [of the intellect]." These lovely and poetic phrases are not mere sophistry. The scientific methods of Sant Mat demonstrate as convincingly as any laboratory test that they are pertinent and objective.

To carry the analogy of the microscope further: in the human apparatus there are also several lenses that have to be brought into proper alignment to obtain the clarity of vision taught to be desirable by seers of all ages. These lenses are the bodies surrounding the soul—physical, astral and mental or causal. And since, as has been said, God cannot reveal Himself to the contaminated mind, it is also obligatory to clean these lenses of the self to get results. As the Bible says, "Blessed are the pure in heart, for they shall see God." This cleansing is perhaps the most difficult of all endeavours and certainly one of the most important functions of any religious exercise, no matter of what denomination.

The other points of the analogy are also important to follow if our inner vision is to be properly focused: the emotions are to be stilled, all distractions and interruptions are to be avoided, and prejudices must be removed or set aside, for there is much that is strange and wonderful to be revealed and then to be silently contemplated. At such time, there is no place for the jangle of intellectual speculation or for theological niceties. Nothing less than complete freedom from mental activity and emotional tension will suffice. This can only be done by correct meditation.

A second useful analogy comes from a familiar phenomenon of everyday life. The agitation and restless rippling of the surface of a river or lake by even the gentlest of winds destroys the transparency of the water that exists in stillness; the entire perception of the life beyond the agitated surface is obscured. Although we can no longer observe that life, it has not been done away with, but it remains in mysterious seclusion until the agitation ceases. The agitation of the mind, like the wind, is the key factor in blanketing our perceptions. As long as the mind runs free, we will have as much success in trying to observe the mysterious, limitless heights through the barriers of emotional and intellectual restlessness as a fish trying to see the sky through water clouded by the action of wind and waves.

There are many yogas and other meditational practices that strive for stillness, some with differing objectives such as developing will power or promoting health. But the art and practice of increased awareness is the basis of them all. Since we are assured by all religions that the kingdom of heaven is inevitably to be seen within, and that to go inside is the right and only way to find genuine emancipation and lasting stability and happiness, we should be sure to choose the right technique of going inside. This right way of going inside, the saints insist, needs a living Master's guidance.

9

GOD-MAN RELATIONSHIP

Following the two admonitions "Know thyself" and "Be still, and know that I am God" in that order is a natural sequence because, as Maharaj Charan Singh says in *Light on Sant Mat*, "Self-realization is but a step to God-realization," which is the true aim of this human life. It is in pursuit of this high objective that many of the oddest pieces of the jigsaw puzzle of life fall logically into place. Fitting any one piece, even a small one, may allow a large pile of others to follow easily. As the picture becomes larger and the theme is revealed, the tangle between victim and culprit and between fate and free will is straightened out.

In this lofty pursuit of what one could call the true God-man relationship, we are reminded again and again by the Sant Mat Masters of the law of karma, of our responsibility for our own sowing and reaping, the result of which is the predicament in which we find ourselves. To enable us to deal with that predicament and to extricate ourselves from the bonds of karma, they give the clearest and most explicit personal instructions.

On our search for self- and God-realization, *Light on Sant Mat* says:

> Even if one has to spend his whole life on research alone, it is not time lost but time gained,

> because the stronger foundation will bring a sound structure. It is, therefore, essential that before accepting Sant Mat principles, the enquiry and investigation should be complete and thorough.
>
> After you have made up your mind, the enquiry should be abandoned and the knowledge applied to practical experiences. This physical body is a rare privilege and opportunity because the main object of life, which is self-realization, can be attained in this human body. We have to carry out the duties of the worldly life and to live as normal human beings, but the goal and destination must not be overlooked.

There is a wide field in the world for this preliminary investigation, and during our search, we should remember this caution. Religions are not that which we believe, but the approach to that which we believe. They are the "proprietary vehicles in which we travel towards our spiritual destination." But the means are so often mistaken for the end that the vehicle and its other occupants become more real than the destination, i.e., God-realization.

Some philosophers of materialism and many atheists claim that religion is only a soporific for the masses or for tired and worn out people, or that spiritual philosophy is only for old folks—a kind of last minute apology, a preoccupation for senile minds. Of this attitude Maharaj Sawan Singh, the saintly sage of Beas who was adored by followers both old and young, says:

> There are many who like to discuss philosophy in the abstract but care little for putting that same philosophy into practice. This is human nature expressing both its strength and weakness. The strength lies in the fact that man, although in practice finds himself weak and incapable of executing

what he wills, yet perseveres in seeking that something, the attainment of which will make him strong and happy. He is an eternal seeker and in all his wanderings in transmigration has been in search of what he lacks. His discussion of philosophy is his innate urge to seek light.

The weakness lies in that in his long wandering he has almost lost his capital and is bankrupt now, too weak to stand unaided on his legs. He was soul at one time when he was in intimate touch with the Word. That was long, long ago when he was in spiritual regions. When the soul lost touch with the Word and associated with the mind in the mind planes, the jewel was thrown away and the imitation grasped. The debased coin could pass as genuine on the mental planes only but is not acceptable in the spiritual planes. The access to the spiritual planes was thus debarred.

The coin was further debased when mind and soul left the mind planes and associated with gross matter in the physical plane. Here the jewel is no longer traceable, man has no knowledge of soul and very poor knowledge of mind.

The coin has become spurious and has no purchasing power in the markets of the mental and spiritual planes. Soul has been materialized, and human nature has become very weak. Therefore, people talk of philosophy and are too weak to put it in practice unaided. They need a living "Christ" not only to rebaptize them with the Word, but to help them both by precept and example.

Spiritual Gems

These words are definite and specific, instead of vague and general, and the Masters are the living example of what they speak. The substance of their philosophy is the Word, which can be practised only under the guidance of a living Master or "Christ."

10

RUBBER STAMPED AT BIRTH

With most of us, our sect or religion—our vehicle for spiritual realization—is an accident of birth; it depends upon the traditions of the nation and the family into which we are born. We are, so to speak, rubber stamped at birth by one or another of the many proprietary establishments. We thus start with a strong and sometimes rigid bias—a bias so unbending as to cause religious wars—to a particular book of rules and precepts.

According to many of these holy books, the accident of birth is no accident at all but happens according to the doctrines of karma and reincarnation (transmigration or resurrection).[1] The following list names a few of the traditional repositories of the teachings of the great mystics and indicates their antiquity and disparate sources.

Granth Sahib—Sikhism: 400 years old; follow Nanak and nine other saints

Quran—Islam: 1,300 years old; follow Mohammed

New Testament—Christianity: 1,900 years old; follow Christ

---

[1]The perversion of these teachings can be seen in many religious rituals. In ancient Egypt, mummification preserved the body for the reincarnation or return of the soul. In one Christian burial custom, the congregation or laity are interred west-east and the parson or priest laid east-west so that at the sound of the last trumpet they can arise facing each other.

Tao Te Ching—Taoism: 2,500 years old; follow Lao-tse

Zend Avesta—Zoroastrianism: 2,500 years old; follow Zarathustra

Vedas—Hinduism: 3,500 years old; follow various sages

Tripitaka—Buddhism: 2,500 years old; follow Buddha

Old Testament—Judaism: 3,000 years old; follow Moses and other prophets

Book of the Dead—ancient Egyptian: 6,000 years old

The original aim of these writings was not just to lay down a code of morals and conduct for an indifferent and unheeding mass of humanity, but to develop the disciple's inner and higher consciousness, in other words, to promote God-consciousness. That this has never been easy is apparent, for we are told that "many are called, but few are chosen." That this has never been popular is also apparent, for the saints who teach God-realization have often become "despised and rejected of men." History records the hideous martyrdom meted out to so many of those noble souls who sought to enlighten mankind.

> Jesus Christ was nailed to the cross. Mansur was tortured to death. Shamas-i-Tabriz was flayed alive. Guru Nanak was put to hard labour. Guru Arjun was made to sit on hot iron plates and in cauldrons of boiling water. Guru Teg Bahadur was beheaded. All of these great Masters came to redeem us and we tortured them. What heights of sheer ingratitude!
>
> *Discourses on Sant Mat*,
> Maharaj Sawan Singh

History also shows the interference, conscious or otherwise, with the pure and lofty teachings of these sages, first through the inability of lesser minds to appreciate the depth and immensity of their vision; then through the inaccuracies of retelling and translation; still further through opportunism, ritualism, politics and vested interests; and finally through the changing idiom of the times. It is not easy to plumb the depths of degradation meted out to their exalted ideals, which were based entirely upon the teaching of love. Their grand truth that man is able to unite with God here and now is often reduced to a vague promise of life with God hereafter, providing that one observes the proper rituals and taboos.

A short perusal of James G. Frazer's *The Golden Bough* will show that it has been the way of all religions of all ages to twist the truth by dogmatic practices, rituals and superstition. Each religion begins with the same pure vein of gold, but human fallacies and fantasies soon have them straining in opposite directions with different interpretations of the words of the prophets. In all religions, there are theologians and ritualists who are skilled in confusing the issue. But in spite of orthodoxy, in spite of the many antagonistic schools of theology, there is still a chance for that precious thing for which each saint stood; namely, the growth of man's awareness of the inner life through mystic experiences.

There are millions of religious people in the world, and although not many of them adopt the life of a mystic, it is still fair to say that religion is to mysticism what arithmetic is to higher mathematics. The one is far more powerful than the other and has of necessity adopted a different language and outlook, but from the one may develop the other. And so, in the metamorphosis of some, there is an exalted stage at which one revolts against complex intellectual dogma. Of these rebels against sectarian theologies it can be said that "he who can fly is not contained by garden walls; he sees many gardens."

All the greatest messiahs, teachers, magi and gurus were themselves rebels against orthodoxy. They all taught that mystic experiences do not depend upon theological knowledge or ritual but require one-pointed devotion and love coupled with incessant practice. True mystics, no matter what their background, understand each other because they have reached oneness in realizing God.

11

SANT MAT HISTORY

Sant Mat has been taught by its great Masters since the end of the last century at the Radha Soami Colony in Beas, India. Although it is the sole theme of this book, it was not included in the foregoing list of some of the great religions and their scriptures because Sant Mat is not a religion. It has no priests, no temples, no churches or places of pilgrimage. It is an all-embracing science-philosophy, rich as a gold mine for those interested in the emancipation of the soul. It amplifies rather than clashes with existing religions, increasing one's understanding of their prophets, for it is the basis and essence of all religions. As the Masters say, it is the oldest teaching on earth. But it is a new presentation of the changeless, eternal truths for modern needs.

What is the answer to these needs? A practical and simple approach to the highest states of superconsciousness—i.e., self-realization and God-realization—that can be followed within a busy life.

As for the question, How do I seek God-realization, all of the plentiful Sant Mat literature on the subject is put in capsule form by the words, quoted earlier, of Maharaj Charan Singh: "First comes the Grace of God, then the company of Saints and then the acquisition of the secret of Nam. Then by constant application and unceasing devotion, comes the actual realization of Nam. That is the order." First must come the longing for man's lofty inheritance above this miasmic life, then the happy company of the Master or his disciples, then instruction and initiation by him on how to contact the creative Sound, then devotion to meditation. It is the diligent practice of meditation that takes one within to the sacred place of God.

In the light of Sant Mat teachings, one can see that it is misleading to regard the holy men and miracles of religion, as we so often do, in terms of once upon a time or in days gone by. We need not hope desperately for some speculative salvation in a vague life hereafter. The mystic experiences described in the holy books of all religions are still available. They are not illusory or fanciful but are practical and real, and they are attainable here and now. With the expert guidance of a living Master, they can be tried and tested at every step during one's lifetime.

> The inner spiritual progress is sought to be achieved with the help of the Guru or Master who keeps in touch with the disciples through the Shabd or divine harmony within, also called the WORD or Logos.
>
> *Light on Sant Mat*,
> Maharaj Charan Singh

Indeed, spiritual experiences must be attained, at least to some extent, while in this human form. Although Plutarch is correct when he says that "At the moment of death the soul experiences the same impressions, passes through the same process as those who are initiated into great mysteries," he speaks only of the first step of the spiritual journey. The higher spiritual regions and union with God are attainable only by those who, in their lifetime, have practised meditation under the guidance of a living Master. Not until such karma as we bear is dissolved by meditation, not until our debts are honourably discharged, are we perfectly free to stay in realms higher than matter, free from reincarnation. Only then does death—which is never to be feared in the first place because it is merely an episode, like birth, in the life of a soul—become the final liberation from the material world.

The practice of Sant Mat offers true spiritual navigation. The Word or Logos, the audible Sound Current, when caught and listened to by the disciple, is the directional radar that steers the listener through the fogs of intellectual arguments, around emotional storm centres and past the mirages created by egotism. With its aid, one can at any time take soundings of the rocks and shallows of the journey through life and thus not only avoid disaster, but make substantial progress toward his true home, no matter what may be his earthly situation.

All true Masters throughout the ages have taught the same essential spiritual truth, often in parable or metaphor. But after their passing, time and the human factor have buried them under corroding layers of dogma and ritual until many of the vital points are lost or pass unrecognized. Sant Mat has removed the dross from these teachings once again.

The story of Sant Mat is as simple and unsophisticated as is the great philosophy itself. To aid the reader in the brief history that follows, a list of the Radha Soami Masters or Gurus is given here:

1. Swami Ji: b. 1818, d. 1878
2. Jaimal Singh (Baba Ji): b. 1839, d. 1903
3. Sawan Singh (the Great Master): b. 1858, d. 1948
4. Jagat Singh: b. 1884, d. 1951
5. Charan Singh: b. 1916

In the nineteenth century in the city of Agra was born and lived a Hindu named Seth Shiv Dayal Singh. After passing his early life in study and meditation upon the teachings in the Granth Sahib (the bible of Sikhism) and upon the writings of various masters, both Hindu and Muslim, he became widely known as Swami Ji, a great mystic.

It was in Agra in 1861 that he began to expound a practical method, for householders as well as sadhus and ascetics, of consciously reuniting the soul with its origin, the Lord. He called his teachings Sant Mat, and they also became known as the Radha Soami path because of his constant references to Radha Soami, meaning Lord of the soul.

The second Master of Sant Mat, Baba Jaimal Singh, was born in the Punjab in 1839. Even as a child, he moved in search of a Master who could elucidate his spiritual problems. At the age of 18, his quest took him to Agra, for he had learned from an ascetic of the great spiritual powers of Swami Ji. Under the latter's guidance, he attained the profound spiritual state that the Buddhists call samadhi. Even so, he was not allowed to remain with Swami Ji but was directed to carry out one of the essential rules of the teaching—to earn his own living so that he need not be dependent upon others. He thereupon joined the army unit stationed at Agra.

During his military service, he was sent to campaign with his regiment on the northwest frontier, and as his own beloved disciple, later to be Huzur Maharaj Sawan Singh, relates:

> while there, he would at night go out into the open and dig a small pit in the sandy soil. With his rifle tucked behind his knees, he would sit there in meditation the whole night. In the morning the enemy (the Pathans) would be found sitting around him. As he would get up to leave for his regiment, they would pay him respect and obeisance. Nobody would disturb him, and they would say among themselves: "He is a Faqeer. We should not touch him."
>
> *Spiritual Gems*

Recalling his late Master, Maharaj Sawan Singh said, "There are so many wonderful things about Baba Ji that if I go on relating them for one hundred years, it would not be possible to finish them all."

After retirement in 1891, Baba Ji proceeded northwards to the Beas river, one of the five rivers of the Punjab, on whose banks more than one thousand years before Christ a rishi called Vyas (or Beas) had lived and meditated. At this place, where Baba Ji meditated for years in a hut, the present day Radha Soami Colony, also known as Dera Baba Jaimal Singh, grew up.

On the death of Baba Ji in 1903, the mystic teaching was continued for forty-five years by his great disciple Huzur Maharaj Sawan Singh, who had also earned his living in the army as an engineer, qualifying at the Roorkee College of Engineering. The story of Baba Sawan Singh's meeting with Baba Ji in the Murrie Hills, his initiation and spiritual training and his later ministrations is amazing to hear. His mastership spanned the terrible period of the partition of India and Pakistan when the colony at Beas became a veritable oasis for thousands of refugees of every religion. To handle this great influx, the Master, with deep insight, had begun preparing several years before.

Here are two simple but profound stories from amongst the many hundreds told at Beas about the abounding love and spiritual achievement of Baba Sawan Singh. One hot day, a stranger travelling on foot along the dusty road near Beas, unsure of his direction, saw an elderly man sitting with eyes closed, meditating at the roadside. To gain his attention, the traveller tapped him unceremoniously upon the forehead and said he was looking for the hut of a famous Guru in the neighbourhood. Did the man know him?

The traveller was told that the house he was looking for was not far down the road and that if he went there in the afternoon about four o'clock, he would doubtless see the Master he was looking for. At the time stated, the traveller duly turned up at the house only to find his same elderly informant, surrounded by his disciples, in discourse.

Naturally he was deeply embarrassed to find that he had treated the great Guru in such a disrespectful manner, and he was profuse in his apologies. The Master's reply was characteristic: "Oh, my friend, you need not be so worried. If you go to the bazaar to buy an earthenware water jug costing one anna, you tap it to see that it is not cracked. So if you are seeking a Guru, you have the right to test him also."

The second story also concerns a visiting stranger. This man had quietly listened to the Master's teaching at satsang, but after a while he rose and interrupted the discourse, saying that he did not believe that the speaker was a true Guru and implying that he was an impostor.

The astonished disciples became angry and were about to throw him out, whereupon Maharaj Ji quieted them with a gesture of restraint, saying, "Why are you angry with this man? He is entitled to his opinion and I am not angry, so why should you be?"

Thereupon the stranger threw himself at the Master's feet and confessed: "I have been travelling for many years in search of a Satguru. I have tried this harsh trick upon many who claimed to be true saints, and they have always been very angry. Each time I have thought, 'so you have not yet overcome the five enemies, of which anger is one, and are therefore no master of yourself.' And I have gone away knowing that I have yet to find a true Master. Only now have I found one who is without anger or bitterness. I have at last found a true saint."

Before his death in 1948 at age 90, Baba Sawan Singh's initiates included rich and poor, followers of many religions and citizens of many countries.

From his passing until 1951, the fast-growing colony was presided over by Sardar Bahadur Jagat Singh Ji, a retired Professor of Agriculture at Lyallpur. A Master of deepest insight, as shown in his book *The Science of the Soul*, he was much loved by his followers.

Since his death, the Dera has been in the care of the beloved Master, Maharaj Charan Singh Ji. In his teaching, the present Master draws on many saints from the past—like Guru Nanak, Kabir, Tulsi Sahib and Christ—but he always uses language understandable to the modern ear.

In the long history of the world, many beloved holy men have come and gone. The point of this brief history of Sant Mat is that they are to be found today, in the idiom of the time, by a serious and fortunate seeker.

> We in this world have many imperfections and are consequently unhappy and miserable. Our descent here is for purposes which would appear to be wholly remedial. When we have grown clean, strong, brave and God-like, the Almighty Father looks for our return to the homeland. For this purpose He sends His beloved sons whom we may call Masters. Their mission is to take us back to the Holy feet of the divine Supreme Being. Inscrutable providence, the unique power of the Lord, is ever at work.

But how can one recognize a Master? By what outer signs can one expect to distinguish him from other men of stature?

With the passage of time, nearly all established religions have enclosed their teachers in a shrine of reverence embroidered with fantasy and coloured with stories of unique mystic experiences or miracles. It is easy to think romantically of Jesus on a hot day, riding along a dusty road upon a donkey or stopping to drink at a well, or of Buddha quietly meditating in the shade of a pipal tree, or of Mohammed escaping across the desert from Mecca upon a camel, or of Krishna discoursing to his disciple Arjuna. A man on a donkey, a sage under a tree and the like were such ordinary and unromantic happenings, especially in the East, that if one had been a passer-by, it is fairly certain that he would not have noticed anything unusual or of any mystic significance. Indeed, none of the Masters were recognized during their lifetime except by a very few with insight.

The present beloved Master, known affectionately as Maharaj Ji, is fond of driving a car; he does not disdain using air travel; he has a lively sense of humour; he loves children; and he provides the most generous but beautiful and simple hospitality to the seeker who is fortunate enough to gain his company. He rarely uses the word "I"; he does not proclaim himself or advertise; his demeanour is faultless yet not unnatural; he is tireless in his work; and he never shows anger in spite of tremendous provocation at times. Under no circumstances does he accept any gifts. Like you and me, he requires physical sustenance. He does not dress differently, so that one might pass him in a street without notice.

In other words, your ability to recognize him is brought about by more than casual circumstances. As he himself says, it is ordained from past karma.

12

LISTENING TO THE CREATIVE SOUND

> Sant Mat is the practical part of self-realization, and . . . the Inner Sound Current is the essential part of Sant Mat . . . . One is put into contact with this Sound Current by a Master—a Realized Soul—who is himself well versed in it.
>
> *Light on Sant Mat*,
> Maharaj Charan Singh

Sant Mat teaches that the Holy Spirit or Word that so often seems remote and unreal is, in fact, the closest and most reliable part of our existence. It is always present, but it is like butter in milk, which cannot be had without the proper processing, or like a seed in the ground, which cannot grow to maturity without the correct conditions. It is therefore necessary, if one is pursuing the inner path, to have a living Master or Satguru who is qualified to guide the pupil in creating the right conditions for that life force to emerge.

The life force is referred to by so many different names that it is well, in spite of some repetition, to mention a few. In Christian teachings, of course, it is called the Word, the Logos and the Holy Spirit. It is Ism-i-Azam of Muslims, the Nad of the Vedas, and the Sraosha of Zoroastrianism. In the teachings of Lao-tse it is called Tao; in Hinduism it is known as Bani.

All these religions mention the creative Sound, but they fail to realize its vital significance or to teach its practice, even though, as Guru Nanak has said, "By hearing the Word is acquired the wisdom of all Scriptures."

In Sant Mat, the creative factor is known as Nam or Shabd. It is the basis of the highest meditation and the means whereby the soul can regain its true home.

> The Nam which is so highly praised by the saints is the unspoken Word. It cannot be spoken or written. It is the creator of the universe, not limited to time or space, and is the link between us and the Lord. It is true that by reading scriptures we learn of this treasure, but effort and practice are necessary before we can obtain it . . . . Therefore, the true form of worship which is always acceptable to the Lord is Shabd abhyas (practice). All else continues to bind us in this vast prison house of good and evil karmas. We have to contact the Word, which is resounding within the temple of the living God.
>
> *Discourse*,
> Maharaj Charan Singh

The "temple of the living God" is, of course, one's body.

In Sant Mat, the Word—the eternal, ever present, creative Sound Current—is the very core of spiritual practice. It is not something remote but a perceptible vibration resounding in all things and in all men, whether good or bad, wilful or submissive, rich or poor, and of whatever colour. This Sound, which Kabir refers to as pure white music, can be heard by anyone who cares to follow the prescribed method for listening to the voice of silence: "He that hath ears to hear, let him hear."

The music of the Shabd is distant and unsteady when first heard, but as it deepens, it lifts the listener into a hitherto unknown peace. For most of us, it seems, the sounds are perceived only after much practice. There are, however, many accounts of humble and simple people who, upon receiving initiation, spontaneously achieve the faculty of hearing the Sound in varying degrees. These privileged ones have made spiritual advancement in previous incarnations. Their very saintliness and humility indicate their great degree of detachment from the things that bind us to this earth. However long it takes to hear the Shabd, the experience is not as rare as it might seem, even in the West, for disciples are enjoined from discussing their inner experiences lest it lead to pride.

The sound of the Shabd is like a constant theme with variations on all levels. These variations are described as the rushing of a mighty wind, the sound of a lute, the deep resonance of a bell or conch, or the tinkling of glass in the wind. There are also wonderful lights and radiance to accompany the sounds, as inferred by Kabir's description of pure white music. The sounds and lights progress in a definite order, corresponding to each stage of the journey inwards, and they clearly indicate the disciple's progress.

Nearly all these sounds and lights are imitated by religious orders. The familiar church organ, chimes, temple bells and gongs and the altar lights, candles and various lamps are, or should be, but a reminder of those things to be sought in the real inner sanctuary of the human body. For the mystic, they are manifested there with infinitely greater power and beauty.

The reason Masters refer to Sant Mat as a scientific philosophy may now be understood. By raising the attention in meditation and going within, a disciple may prove the existence of the higher spiritual planes claimed by all saints. He can authenticate the inner experiences and manifestations again and again because the signposts of sounds and lights are always the same. These experiences and the presence of a living Master make the previously remote religious teachings, the romanticized, supersensory experiences and the glories of other centuries become personal, practical and, above all, proven.

Some followers of orthodox religions have said that there is nothing new in Sant Mat, for they recognize many familiar features up to a point. But the various religions have quite divergent beliefs and practices. This is misleading because the saints have always had the same message and the same objective, which is to enlighten us with regard to our daily lives, to death itself and to our relationship with other realms of life.

> Rituals and rites . . . , the ceremonial parts of every religion differ according to the customs of the age, and climates and conditions of the countries; but the real Essence of Truth, the Spirituality at the foundation of all religions is the same. They all lead us to the Holy Sound, the Word, the Logos, by hearing which we attain Salvation.
>
> *Light on Sant Mat*,
> Maharaj Charan Singh

The Masters confirm that they give us nothing

new, since they teach the eternal truths that all saints have taught to their disciples. What they point out is that reading books or listening to lectures, sermons and discourses cannot confirm those truths as does the practice of the Sound Current within.

With Sant Mat, the practice of going within is essential, because by it, the disciple becomes familiar with the channels of direct contact with the Master, and he eventually attains the true spiritual awakening of passing through the third eye. The Masters say there is no other way to realize God.

> All feeling of sorrow and grief leaves us when we practise Shabd, for then our ego and desires are curbed. Once we are aware that all possessions belong to the true owner, the Lord himself, and eliminate the I-ness, we have begun to pierce through the wall between us and the Lord.
>
> Maharaj Charan Singh

We all have some understanding of the experiences of an aviator. Having slipped the shackles of earth, he has an immense feeling of freedom. And from the skies, he has a vastly superior perspective of the earth than even those on mountaintops. When he returns to earth, he will not forget his altered consciousness. What is more, he can repeat his experiences again and again.

How much greater, then, the passing at will of the consciousness into inner realms of greatly enhanced freedom! It can be seen that such endeavour is not selfless, but neither is it selfish. It is the kind of thing that the best in everyone aspires to because if it is attained, it must inevitably render service to all.

The disciple's progress on the inward journey is, at all times, in the hands of the Master. And through his love, which is manifestly present at all times, each traveller on the path will eventually reach his destination.

13

INNER EXPERIENCE—RETICENCE

In this peculiar world of ours, with its strangely inverted values, the time and effort devoted to some worldly objective such as athletic or intellectual prowess is universally applauded, whereas the time and effort spent on spiritual matters is begrudgingly given. But the former produces only fleeting material results and more karmic attachments. The exact opposite is true for those who, following the first essential teaching of Sant Mat, accept a living Master. From him, an entirely new concept of action in serenity is drawn. With his help and love, which is assured at all times (even at a disciple's death he is present in his astral or radiant form), conflicts begin to subside, and the results of a disciple's spiritual efforts are permanent and eternal.

One of the greatest advantages of having a living Master is that, wherever you may be, you have his active guidance, for it is possible to consult him in person or by letter. There are also an increasing number of books in English—such as *Spiritual Gems*, *The Science of the Soul* and *Light on Sant Mat*—that are partly composed of the Masters' answers to disciples' letters. They cover the whole field of intimate problems that the aspirant meets in his daily efforts to keep to his practices. But the depth and understanding of the replies, which are in the Masters' own words, are like balm to others who encounter similar difficulties.

It should be clear by now that the Master is not regarded as an ordinary man, nor does the Western concept of a saint properly describe him. Neither is he regarded as a sadhu or yogi, both of which terms are often loosely or erroneously used. There are, especially in the East, so many sadhus of such differing calibre that the greatest discretion is called for if one is seeking a Master.

It is not altogether easy for a Westerner to understand the relationship between a Satguru and his *chelas* or pupils; it is so close and intimate a bond. Just how close it can be, in spite of great distances and trying circumstances, must be experienced to be truly understood. But perhaps an analogy will help to illustrate the relationship.

If one aspires to ascend a mountain peak, he must undertake some important preliminaries. Although the climb cannot be done by reading books, these, of course, provide helpful information. Then one must train, both physically and mentally. And the journey to the starting point must be taken.

But the most critical step is to seek a reliable guide; not one who offers his advice or wears some badge or uniform yet who has little skill in the intricacies of the climb, for he will be no better than a fellow traveller. Nor does one seek a guide who just points to the route or talks at great length about the climb. One needs a guide who, having completed the climb many times himself, is personally intimate with every step and every pitfall along the way, because one's very life is entrusted to him. This much, and very much more, does the *chela* rely upon his Satguru. Otherwise, his effort is fruitless.

If the mountain guide accepts you as his charge, he will insist upon your travelling light, stripped of every unnecessary accoutrement. One must travel the inner ascent similarly unburdened. The Masters insist upon the utmost simplification, as we may read. Two thousand years ago Christ said to the young and richly attired aspirant who was powerfully attracted by the prospect of the lofty inner journey: "If you would be perfect, go, sell what you possess . . . and come, follow me." He meant, "Give up a false sophisticated life of distractions and follow my instructions."

Two thousand five hundred years ago, according to the legends of the Buddha's life, the noble Prince Siddhartha stripped himself of his princely trappings and wandered as a beggar for many years in search of enlightenment—only to find it within himself.

But the modern technique of the Masters is attuned to more modern needs. It is concerned with self-discipline, yes, but not with ascetic penances such as starvation, wearing a hairshirt and other mental and bodily tortures followed by ancient yogic schools. The Masters point out that those practices continually draw our attention out to the needs and wants of body and mind, the very things from which we eventually must become detached. The more we become detached and impersonal towards them and attached to the Sound Current, the more easily do we toil and the more graciously do we accept our karmas. When the time comes for us to die, we pass without struggle or regret, because the route our soul takes after death is the same one that it has been travelling daily.

Of the spiritual powers and detachment developed by the many types of yogas, there is much misapprehension, both in the East and West. They give powers by control and concentration—powers that may be used for good and bad. Of this there is no doubt whatsoever. But these powers are not by any means inherently holy or sacred.

The author has met a number of accomplished yogis, *sanyasis* and sadhus. With some of them the renunciation of name, home and worldly possessions was but a magnificent gesture. They gloried somewhat arrogantly in their powers, which provided them, as one of them said, with the best of everything, such as good food and lodging. Their attitudes displayed considerable ego and little humility. This must not be construed as a general condemnation or criticism of yoga, but as a warning that the credulity of the West has been and is still being freely exploited by some who grossly misuse their powers under the guise of spirituality.

To be in this world but not of it—to be like a duck on the water that flies away with dry wings—is the advice of the Masters. They advocate detachment not as an end in itself, but as a means to an end. Detachment from material and mental considerations is preparation for attachment to the Sound Current.

This attachment is achieved by the second essential of Sant Mat, the practice of raising the attention to the inner eye through concentration, as instructed by the Master at initiation. One must practise constantly, whether idle or busy, because listening to the unspoken Word is purifying. It transports us sooner or later from our slum lodgings to the mansions of our true heritage in Sach Khand, our divine home.

Once a disciple has gained the inner regions, a third essential teaching comes to bear—that of reticence. Contrary to most religions, the followers of Sant Mat are warned not to discuss with others any inner experiences they may have or to advertise this evidence of the Master's grace. This feature of reticence sometimes puzzles inquirers and newcomers, but there are good reasons for it.

The greatest danger of relating one's experience is that it may lead to pride or egotism (chaffingly called "holy blight"), which is one of the five perversions of the mind. Humility is utterly essential for inner progress because egotism chokes our ability to be receptive to anything but our own minds. It is therefore highly detrimental to spiritual progress to be indiscreet about inner experiences.

Also, there is the possibility that experiences might be compared, which could discourage one who has not made as much progress as another. Other perils of disclosure are gossip and exaggeration for the purpose of dramatization.

Still another reason that experiences should be closely held is that, as the Masters point out, anyone who is persuaded to follow a faith because of reported spiritual phenomena or miracles, however beautiful, is not following from inner conviction and may later be easily led astray. Some of these experiences may also be mental in origin—told by a disciple who has not reached the third eye—and therefore not reliable. For all these reasons, disciples come to appreciate the aphorism, "Silence is golden."

14

MAN IS THE TOP OF CREATION, BUT—?

With all the fabulous scientific achievements of the twentieth century, it may seem strange to some to realize that the possibility of an inner life, of listening to the Word in meditation, is not relegated to the past but is as real today as in any era. The fact that physical transportation is now by train, car and jet does not invalidate the age-old teaching of how to reach the inner realms. The fact that our material standard of living may have improved does not alter in any way the facts of the inner journey. The technique of seeking has always been the same. It has just been lost in vague or meaningless ritual.

In 1950, Sardar Bahadur Jagat Singh wrote these words:

> Man is the top of all creation, the perfect handiwork of Nature in all respects. He contains within himself the key to unlock the mystery of the Universe and to contact the Creator. It is the greatest and highest good fortune of any sentient being to be born in the form of a man.
>
> But his responsibilities are also correspondingly great. Having come up to the top of the evolutionary ladder, he should now step on to the ladder of NAM and tread the Spiritual Path that will ultimately lead him to the Divine Home whence he came....

Huzur Maharaj Sawan Singh giving satsang

View over the Radha Soami Colony in the Punjab, showing Beas River in flood and snow-capped Himalavas in the distance

Maharaj Charan Singh during satsang

Volunteer workers erecting a retaining wall on the river bank for reclaimed ground with some living quarters as a part of the wall

During a discourse in a village, Maharaj Charan Singh gestures towards the vital point of consciousness

Author, wife and friend

A crevasse is filled by the basket load at seva

Makers of Parshad

Maharaj Charan Singh arrives to give satsang

Maharaj Charan Singh
inspecting work done
by volunteers

Satsang at the Radha Soami colony

Maharaj Charan Singh oversees seva

Temporary accomodation at the bhandara
meetings, attended by 200,000 or more

> In the human body, the eye centre is the spot which represents the end of one course and the beginning of the other. Man may go up or he may slide down.
>
> This is the message which all Saints and Masters have given to the world, in their own time....
>
> The first step towards Spiritual practice is to understand the object of hearing the Shabd. The function of Shabd is to lift the soul upwards and inwards, to the higher planes.
>
> *The Science of the Soul*

Some parts of this statement may be unfamiliar and even uncomfortable to the Western ear. A discriminating mind, however, can often find in Western doctrines the vestigial remains of these same tenets. The scars of censorship and misinterpretation have marred, but not completely erased, the original teachings. They have, however, left significant gaps in our rationale. One of these misinterpretations is the belief in the resurrection of the body, which is surely a distortion or misrepresentation of reincarnation. Another misinterpretation is of the law of karma (an eye for an eye, a tooth for a tooth), which is often considered to be the cruel code of conduct that people were taught to live by before the time of Christ. Another widely misunderstood teaching is that of transmigration or metempsychosis. All these things are more easily understood in the light of Sant Mat and do much to explain the pattern of life.

After going through the intellectual exercise of clarifying ancient religious tenets, one needs to ask: how do they affect the picture that I have started to build from the rough pieces of my life? What contribution do they make to the resolution of my own predicament?

We are forced to admit, if we accept the law of karma, that we are responsible for what happens to us, good or bad—that we are both victim and culprit. As the Christian prayer book says, we have done those things that we ought not to have done, and we have left undone those things that we ought to have done. There is no "health" in us: we are "miserable sinners."

Christian Science says that our misfortunes are due to error and wrong thinking. Eastern philosophy agrees, saying that our karma is the result of mind and maya (illusion). All karma, good or bad, is the result of our thoughts and actions. Wrong and irresponsible thinking produces wrong acting and vice versa.

But when did we commit the act whose effects we are now feeling? In this life? In one of our many past lives? In both? The Masters say that our circumstances are the summation of cause and effect, acting and reacting, sowing and reaping, over many lives.

Since the law of karma is inexorable, since we must face the results of our actions eventually, is it even expedient to try to avoid our just deserts? Even if one commits a crime and is not found out, it is hardly a matter for self-congratulation. Have we not been told that even the fall of a sparrow is noted? It does us no good, either, to try to pass the responsibility on to others.

Accepting our responsibility is certainly a step towards repentance. As Christ said to his disciples, "If any man would come after me, let him deny himself and take up his cross daily and follow me." But even repentance does not automatically wash away the consequences to us of our actions. For example, if one kills or wounds or robs or otherwise misbehaves, it is not enough to be sorry; repentance does not end the debt of karma attached to the action, although it greatly helps. A debt has in all fairness to be paid to the last grain of wheat. If these facts were stressed in early education, it might have a remarkable effect upon our social system.

In times of trouble, we all pray for forgiveness and mercy. But we are guilty of loose thinking with regard to how much we may expect to be relieved of our self-made burdens of ill health, anxieties and fears. How urgently we need the Master's help to teach us how to face up to our karma. And we are told that a call for his help is never unanswered. The Master will take over that portion of our karma which we cannot avoid, our fate karma, and administer it compassionately, according to our ability to withstand it. But we must be prepared to accept gracefully whatever is obligatory for the sake of our own soul, which the Master, the spiritual *dhobi* or washerman, is endeavouring to cleanse.

In addition to bearing our present karma without complaint, we are instructed to "go, and sin no more" so that we may not increase or prolong our suffering. Naturally, if the sowing continues in the wrong vein, so will the reaping. But fortunately, the sowing can be corrected by the enlightened use of our will, and the reaping, however arduous, can be accepted cheerfully. What cannot be cured must be endured, but what must be endured can be put to good use as a cautionary experience.

It is not easy to admit that you are gathering

your own harvest unless things are going in your favour. Nevertheless, this is the teaching of the Masters. But they also clearly indicate the interplay of fate and free will: although your destiny may be immutable, you still have enough will to alter your present sowing and thereby influence your future fate. To that extent you have freedom of action. If you are intent enough on using it, you can ultimately control the domination of the mind by the senses and the domination of the soul by the mind.

The Masters, with their unbounded compassion and patience, assure that justice is administered with mercy. Justice it is, although when it is onerous we may indignantly call it otherwise because we see only part of the picture, forgetting the actions of our past lives. Justice is not something we can judge at this stage, because we are too involved with our present life and have no memory of our past lives.

One may protest, for instance, that as an "innocent" child one was started off on the wrong foot because of bad parents or poverty. Another may be fair enough to admit to the strong advantages of being born into a good family of wealth and position. (From the spiritual point of view, these judgements might be reversed, for in this respect the rich are often poorer and vice versa.) But heredity, which to the Western mind is the reason for much of one's fate, is regarded by the Masters as merely part of that fate. In other words, the circumstances of birth are not accidental.

It is common to blame our misfortunes on parents, grandparents, nurses, doctors, or anyone else who can be a scapegoat, but the law of karma insists that, having by our own actions instigated our own fates, we cannot pass off our responsibility and get away with anything. Our debts follow us from incarnation to incarnation, in the continuum of lives taught by most Eastern philosophies and even by early Christianity.[1] The hunter must repay his debt to the hunted, the torturer to the tortured and the cheat to the cheated; but also, of course, the benefactor will receive benefaction. This is the natural balancing of the inexorable law of karma, not the wrath of God or even punishment.

> Hate breeds hate and love itself,
> It is not chance, 'tis law.

Just as this tiny planet is only a speck in a vast universe, our physical existence is but a small part of the infinite realm of conscious existence. This, again, is taught by all the Saints and Masters. Science supposes that life cannot exist in places without something like our own atmospheric conditions: oxygen, nitrogen, hydrogen and so forth. That, however, is not life in the bigger concept that affirms that life (or God) is everywhere. Why do we persist in a concept of life or consciousness as spatial or three-dimensional? It is incompatible with our talk of absolute oneness with God, life hereafter or universal mind.

Consciousness does not necessarily imply a cellular structure or something that is destructible and therefore temporary. All this is certainly known to men in their superconscious and subconscious states, into both of which they may have a glimpse occasionally.

---

[1]Luke 9, 18–19: " 'Whom say the people that I am?' They answering said, 'John the Baptist; but some say, Elias; and others say that one of the old prophets is risen again.' "

These glimpses are denied to most people in their normal consciousness. During times of stress or heightened awareness, however, such things may be revealed.

We are taught that, since our spirit is indestructible but our life in this world is transitory, we pass on from here to some other place or state of consciousness. If this is so, it is reasonable to suppose that we also come here from some other place or state of consciousness. This is scarcely in dispute, for it is a basic teaching of nearly all religions. The motif of sadness in folk music is caused by nostalgic but subconscious memory of a lost glory that is rightfully ours and that we can regain.

We refer to the place from which we originally came as our Father's house and the Bible speaks of the many mansions therein. Most people think this is only poetic imagery, and they are right, for the mansions represent not three-dimensional buildings but states of consciousness. Direct knowledge of these mansions can be had by following Sant Mat. Only then can we understand why the saints say that in the higher planes we are dead to the material life, and in the material plane we are dead to the spiritual life.

Contrary to Christian belief, we do not come straight from our Father's house at birth and go straight back to it at death. Our soul follows a long process of reincarnation and transmigration represented by the story of the prodigal son and by *Pilgrim's Progress*. When our souls emerged from the Creator, they descended into the realms of mind and matter, each behaving according to its own urges and fancies, each taking its own road through the creation according to the fate set in motion by its actions. This process continues until it is consciously broken by self-realization, which leads to God-consciousness, or union with the Father.

Not until our karmic debts are being consciously balanced, not until our desires for worldly things are being transmuted into spiritual aspirations, can we make any progress homewards. But the journey home is not the preoccupation of just one life or part of one life. Many lifetimes of desires created the chains that bind us to the creation, so it may take more than one lifetime, according to our efforts, to break them.

Because our desires have drawn us back again and again to this level of consciousness, our karmic obligations also belong to this plane. Therefore, it is only on this plane, while in the human form, that our obligations can be fulfilled and our chains can be broken. Struggling uninstructed with our fate, we are as in need of a rescuer as a drowning man. But our rescuer must also be on this plane; that is, we need a living Master or Satguru.

Having contacted such a Master, we can be instructed in the technique of purifying the consciousness and raising it above the storms of mind and emotional stresses while still discharging our karmic reponsibilities and the duties of daily life. We learn to follow the path of devotion or *bhakti*. It is through love and devotion, which becomes so absorbing, that our earthly bonds are eventually broken forever and we are free. Such is the holy purpose of Sant Mat.

15

END TO REINCARNATION

Karma is such a binding influence on our present and future lives, and has so many aspects, that it is worthy of further consideration. The old cliché that marriages are made in heaven is a happy romanticism, but it is nevertheless true, for marriages and all our other karmas are apportioned to us by the lord of karma, the power that prevails in the regions of higher mind, which are often referred to as heaven. Sooner or later, this power brings us together with those to whom we must pay and those from whom we must receive so that the accounts can be settled. These fate karmas are given to us from the great reserve of unpaid accounts (called *sinchit* karma) that we add to with every life.

In *Julius Caesar*, Shakespeare says, "The evil that men do lives after them. The good is oft interred with their bones." But this is not a statement of karma. Neither the good nor the bad is buried with the body. Both may be carried over on the scales of justice into a subsequent life. If they are not fulfilled, the desires and motives by which we are guided or driven and the obligations we incur in this life continue onwards. They bind us to the world with its limited consciousness, causing us to be born again and again in circumstances that will enable us to fulfill them. If our desires are subhuman, then we are wishing a subhuman incarnation upon ourselves, in accordance with the law of transmigration or metempsychosis. This law is the basis of such folklore as vampires and werewolves.

Many people wonder why it is they do not remember their past lives, even though they probably do not even recall their actions and thoughts of last year or last week. However, the characteristics that make us so different from one another, which we explain as heredity, are often the result of the impressions of past lives carried over in our subconscious memory. For the most part, as stated in the introduction to *The Invocation of Sheikh Abdullah Ansara*, the "facts . . . are not within the cognition of those whose consciousness has not been freed from the clouding of the senses." But sometimes these recollections, called *sanskaras*, do percolate through to our consciousness, puzzling the psychiatrist and challenging the rationalist. Occasionally, one may even have a comprehensive picture from a past life, which for lack of a better explanation is usually attributed to something like supersensory perception or clairvoyance.

Sant Mat teaches that full recollection of our past lives occurs at a higher state of consciousness, but only if required for the development of the soul. The conscious recollection of them is mercifully withheld until we are spiritually strong enough to see them in perspective and to profit by the experience. A full recollection of our past deeds and actions, at this stage, would almost certainly be too revealing and perhaps even crippling. We are therefore given the anodyne of forgetfulness of our past incarnations.

Reincarnation constitutes an evolutionary chain in which the debits and credits of fate are made and paid. The links of this chain can be of gold or of iron, depending on whether our actions are good or bad, but they can only be broken with the help of a living Satguru, who shows us how to free ourselves by adhering to the path of devotion.

If we are still lured by the sexual, passionate, cruel life of the underworld, we can experience them again and again, life after life. But as the Satguru says, a snake is only dangerous until its venom is removed. If we ardently wish to defang the snake of desire, to check our descent and begin the ascent home, there is a ready hand outstretched. To repeat the heartening words of the mystics: "When the pupil is ready the Master appears." He shows his outstretched hand in unexpected but unmistakable ways. And ultimately, to his disciples, he shows his radiant form to their inner vision. Then his presence never leaves them.

In their understanding of and infinite compassion for our dilemma, the Masters take charge of their disciples' karma, taking some upon their own shoulders (the much debated vicarious atonement of Christianity) and helping the disciple repay in the best way possible what he cannot avoid—his fate or *pralabdh* karma for this life. Even under a Master's guidance, the karma that provides the right body and fitting environment for our needs cannot be erased.

> The moving finger writes; and, having writ,
> Moves on: nor all your piety nor wit
> Shall lure it back to cancel half a line,
> Nor all your tears wash out a word of it.
>
> *The Rubáiyát of Omar Khayyám*

But the Masters tell us that, although we cannot rid the world of thorns, we can put a stout pair of boots on our feet. The disciple who cooperates willingly and follows a Master's enlightened instructions will find that the effects of his fate karma are lessened. The wind is tempered to the shorn lamb.

To close out his karmic account, the disciple must also burn his store of reserve or *sinchit* karma and refrain from creating new karma to add to it. This is done by putting into practice the words "Thy will be done," by following the path of devotion to full repentance and complete surrender.

The first step toward such surrender happens when the touchstone of meditation begins to turn the mind to gold. The heart quietly begins to vibrate with a different harmony, and on both the physical and mental planes one's life is immensely affected.

This does not mean that life henceforth is a joyride or a bed of roses. But the act of surrender, presupposing as it does that we recognize our responsibility for our debts and desire to set our own world right, gives us a fuller and better sense of values. We now have a new basis from which to see our limited free will more effectively. Life changes into a different gear as one acquires a sense of direction and participation.

Through the devotional exercise of meditation, the disciple develops a more mature consciousness. The low material clouds begin to clear, the emotional morass of this earthly life begins to recede and awareness of life's purpose grows. There comes a willingness, even a keenness, to settle those debts that have held us in thrall and kept our noses to the grindstone of the material world.

> The same mind, which worked through the physical organs of senses with worldly objects, now finds itself in a different world (Anda), far more attractive and stable; looking at which, the mind begins to discard what it had held dear before.
>
> *Spiritual Gems,*
> Maharaj Sawan Singh

Our ego, which Guru Nanak calls a dreadful disease, begins to subside as it is replaced by a growing feeling of union with God. As Maharaj Charan Singh says, "If we cut the root of ego, we are one with God."

As stated before, the Master at Beas teaches a definite technique to be followed by those who yearn to end the wheel of reincarnation, to go beyond the point of no return. But he warns that it is not an easy path. True, it is a path of love, but there are many things to trip up the traveller—shibboleths, conventions, labels, old habits, emotions and conditioned reflexes. All of the five perversions of mind—lust, anger, greed, attachment and egotism—must be confronted and conquered. When we consider that these five perversions have been given expression for many, many lives, we can see that the task ahead is great indeed.

Release from reincarnation is not the escapism that psychologists talk about at length. Both they and mystics know that the idea of escaping from the world, which is often recognized as a prison, is an idle thought. Escape from a prison of bricks and mortar eventually leads to desperation and recapture. It may even lead to an extension of captivity. And so it is with our karma. We cannot escape our responsibilities to family, friends and society by hiding in the mountains or forests.

But escape is one thing, genuine release is another. There is one safe and reasonable way of final release from our obligations, and that is an honourable discharge that has been earned, with possible time off for good conduct. Such honourable release is the whole objective of spiritual endeavour, whether under Sant Mat or under sects and religions. The ultimate purpose is to return home.

The way may be hard and tedious, and it may seem that a fighting, passionate, rebellious spirit could make faster progress, but all the teachings of the saints advise the way of love and humility. The five distortions or perversions of mind have to be conquered systematically, if we are to avoid repeating our old invidious patterns of behaviour. It will require a brave and sustained effort to change the activities and habits of mind that encourage the five perversions. But we learn to recognize them for what they are and to deal with them when we hold to the principles and follow the techniques taught by the Masters.

Most religions do not require the high standard of discipline that Sant Mat requires, but then they do not offer the same inner experience.

> In fact religions of to-day lay stress on moral and social reformation rather than on spiritual enlightenment; they do not reveal God to us, nor impart knowledge of transcendent entities.
>
> *Mysticism, the Spiritual Path,*
> L. R. Puri

A moral or religious person may not necessarily aspire to be a mystic, nor need a mystic belong to any religious body. But a mystic must have self-discipline and a living Master.

16

SPIRIT ENSLAVED BY MIND

The mind is a good servant but a very bad master—so say the saints. Sant Mat teaches that when spirit descended into the material plane, it passed through the region of universal mind. There it picked up association with the mind and, in the course of time, became enslaved by it. This situation was bad enough, but mind itself then became almost entirely preoccupied with its own desires and the distractions of the senses.

One could liken the relationship of spirit and mind to that of a very rich man who engages a manager for his estate. At first the employer is faithfully served, but he is so engrossed with other matters that, after a while, so much authority and routine has been assumed by his deputy that he is no longer master in his own house. Every effort on his part to obtain service is fruitless because the one-time servant is himself now fully preoccupied with affairs of his own.

On the material plane then, the mind is the usurper of power—a ruthless dictator—and is regarded as the authority and as the rightful owner of all it surveys. The former master, the spirit, languishes in frustration behind the bars of our intellect. This domination of the mind prompted the American humourist-philosopher Mark Twain to observe that "Life does not consist mainly or even largely of fact or happenings. It consists mainly of the storm of thought that is forever blowing through one's head."

The great universal unhappiness caused by the soul's eclipse is the reason behind the perpetual unrest and dangers in which we live. Factual knowledge and power are avidly pursued to the virtual exclusion of the greater virtues of wisdom and love. We now have a fantastically high standard of living but a low standard of thinking. We excuse our doubtful and often shameful actions as human nature. But we cannot disguise the soul-destroying cruelty and licentiousness that is subhuman behaviour—well below what we know to be human in the real sense of a perfect man.

These actions incur the heaviest of karmic debts, becoming a millstone around our neck. Some actions are so vile and base that, as Sant Mat teaches, they are incompatible with the human form, which is a great privilege. They cause a reversion to animal or other subhuman form in one's next birth. A reading of Frazer's *Golden Bough* will doubtless convince one of the existence of this law of transmigration.

In a way, we already know it is true; the subconscious mind of man has always contained this conviction, which expresses itself in many ways such as folklore, morality plays and ballet and fairy stories. Mythology is full of the theme of transmigration—animals, birds and even trees being the bodies given to erring humans. Even some old wives' tales have their basis in transmigration and could more correctly be called old wise tales.

The gloomy side of folklore is relieved, of course,

by the happy stories of following the yellow brick road to the great wizard or of being helped by the good fairy. Even from childhood we are also well aware, in our deeper consciousness, of the presence and availability of the Master, the spiritual alchemist.

To repeat, there are some actions that merit and receive a life or lives other than human, not because of the wrath of God, but as a natural working out of the law of cause and effect in the appropriate medium. But transmigration also works in the opposite direction. The human form and privileges can be won back by hard work, by merit and by the grace of God.

One may speculate on the good fortune of the ass that Christ rode into Jerusalem: surely having served a Master it has earned a step upwards and is an animal no longer! And what of all those other well-loved animal friends of man that have devotion in their hearts? Surely they are inheriting something better. And those lovable beasts, the domesticated Indian buffaloes—they are perfect models of resignation. May they not be the reincarnation of arrogant humans—haughty dowagers, cruel kings, queens and dictators of the past, even ourselves—humbly and patiently working out the karma caused by their prideful mistakes? It would not seem impossible.

> The soul is given the body of a cow after passing through the whole gamut of eighty-four lakh species,[1] and then is born as a human being. If one lives a good life, he will continue to be born as a human being till the goal is reached. And by living a good life is meant to keep on remembering

---

[1]A *lakh* equals 100,000. The 8,400,000 species into which a soul might incarnate make up *chaurasi*, the wheel of eighty-four.

> one's exalted origin, for his origin does not change when he transmigrates.
>
> *Sar Bachan*,
> Swami Ji

As we become adults, the expression of our yearning for release, or at least relief, from the treadmill of the daily grind, changes from the whimsical fairy language of our childhood to the poetic search for the Holy Grail. Such a search is recognized as a vital necessity by the deeper layers of man's consciousness. But although we have indications of the visions, the lights and the audible current of heavenly music within—symbolized by the lights and the music of our religious ceremonies—we seldom follow up on these clues to our advantage.

The greater poets certainly render a fine service in their expressions of the higher intuitions but, as already pointed out, reading does not bring personal inner experience of them.

There is a lovely prayer in the present Master's native language, Punjabi, which says: "*Satguru Ji, mohe apna rupa dikhao*"—"Beloved Master, show me thy radiant form."

The Satguru assures us that such experiences are not only within our reach, but that the means of obtaining them are within us, available for daily sustenance as well as for eternity. Again, in the words of Tennyson:

> Speak to Him thou for He hears,
> and Spirit with Spirit can meet:
> closer is He than breathing,
> and nearer than hands and feet.
>
> *The Higher Pantheism*

But as Maharaj Ji says again and again with great

emphasis, it is a practical problem: "*Bhajan karo, Bhajan karo!*"—"Do your meditation," or as it says in the Bible, "Watch and pray." The disciple should let nothing deter him from the daily practice of meditation. As the Master says, it does not interfere with earning one's livelihood, but is truly compatible with it. Indeed, the essence of the meditation permeates the life and livelihood, removing the grievous burdens from it.

If one is dominated by mind, as we mostly are, we can easily worship, as we mostly do, science and material possessions to the *n*th degree, to the complete stultification of the eternal verities. The power of mind over matter is fascinating to pursue until one begins to realize that it does nothing to free one from the deadly cage of the world and has, indeed, forged the bars. What is needed is the power of spirit over both mind and matter, or rather freedom of spirit from both mind and matter. The mind, at any level, is considered by the saints to be negative and illusory as compared to spirit, which is positive and eternal. The teachings of Sant Mat take one above and beyond the realms of the mind, the highest of which is called universal mind or Brahm.

This physical but transient world of nature, of karma, of tooth and claw survival is the domain of the negative power, Mammon or Satan. He works through our mind and senses, which are our weaknesses. His utter self-assurance that temporal power and splendour are his to give and his great confidence in their fatal fascination clearly indicate him to be viceroy of this material world. Only one who has achieved complete detachment from this world could resist such temptation, as did Jesus, when Satan took him "up into a high mountain," showed him all the splendours of his (Satan's) domain, and offered them in return for his allegiance.

There are stories of temptation about Buddha, Zoroaster and Guru Nanak, but they prevailed because, as the Masters say, "Where there is Nam (Holy Spirit) there is no *kam* (lust)" or greed or desire to possess. The opposite, "Where there is *kam* there is no Nam," applies to we lesser ones, who fail the test time after time like Faust, who sold his soul to the devil for knowledge and power. We take Mammon's bait so often that we get the impression we are following the real thing. We are trapped by illusion. Our story is that of *Paradise Lost*, while that of *Paradise Regained* becomes a myth or fable.

But Mammon's powers can be limited by our own integrity. We can use our limited free will to decide which course is to prevail—up or down, paradise regained or lost again, genuine release from prison or back to enslavement, the path of God or the path of Mammon.

Sant Mat says that the mind is the instrument of this long-term imprisonment. It is fascinated and enslaved by endless sense enjoyments and the illusion of power, which it is at great pains to justify. It even gives us a sense of security, false though it may be.[1] The Bhagavad Gita (Song Celestial) says: "The mind which follows the rambling senses makes the soul as

[1]Readers of Dickens will remember the situation of Dr. Manette in the *Tale of Two Cities*. He was in prison for so long that he could not face or even understand freedom, even when his cell door was opened. He only felt secure in his imprisonment and was terrified to leave it.

helpless as the boat which the wind leads astray upon the waters."

It is the mind that builds prisons and hospitals and furnishes them both with inhabitants. It can build a cathedral, then establish a slaughter house, a brothel or an arms factory not far off and still not regard them as being incompatible.

Mind is the great illusionist who, by waving its wand of logic and reason, will make black appear white. It can make almost anything appear rational, yet it can easily become unhinged itself. It can invent time and make it appear both as eternity and something that rules our daily lives hour by hour.

At first, all this castigation of the mind may seem totally unfair and exaggerated. True, when trained and disciplined it can make a wonderful servant, but just watch what happens during any attempt to control it for meditation. It will argue, fidget, rationalize, lie, procrastinate and excuse. It will flatter, cajole or even go to sleep, as Christ's disciples did that night in Gethsemane. Reproving them, he said, "What, could ye not watch [meditate] with me one hour?"

On this subject of mind Maharaj Charan Singh says:

> Mind is the great obstruction which keeps us away from God and pulls us down into this material universe. It is the agent, as it were, of the negative power, and by hook or crook—sometimes posing as a friend and sometimes threatening as an opponent—keeps us involved in this world. It is not easy to come to the Satsang or the society of Gurumukhs, and when one begins to do so the mind presents worldly desires and worldly ambitions and wants them to be fulfilled through their help. This

> is contrary to Bhakti or devotion to God and is devotion to Mammon . . . .
>
> Gurumukhs warn us to beware of the tricks of the mind and to have faith in the words of the Guru. Mind is keen only on affairs of the world and on earning wealth and position. It cares little for Spiritual uplift. It does not like to accept the Sharan of (refuge in) the Satguru because that involves restraint and control.
>
> If we continue to follow the tendencies and dictates of the mind it will only have one result: our coming and going from this world, in one form or another, will never cease.

The worship of mind is at the back of man's problems in this life, which itself is so illusory that Shakespeare says of it, "We are such stuff as dreams are made of . . . ." But does this not also imply that we wake from the dream to find reality? Sant Mat practice, in the hands of the Satguru, makes quite sure that we do wake and discard the dream. But the even more heartening thing is that the awakening can come during this very life. We do not have to await the moment of passing, nor the life hereafter.

It may be that many a doubter, agnostic and even atheist becomes so and remains so because, like some horses, his mind refuses the first jump over what appears to be hazardous or impossible. Many refusals create a habit and a more or less permanent barrier that separates them from those who are willing to surmount.

Although some people who like to call themselves practical or down to earth may still insist that seeking the inner life is escapism, we all, without exception, aspire to a lasting happiness and a freedom that is not found in material values. Christ taught that, to obtain happiness, we should "render unto Caesar the things that are Caesar's; and unto God the things that are God's." In other words, live in this world and follow its rules, but actively seek to reunite our soul with God. And "the kingdom of God," Christ said, "is within you."

Could anything be clearer? Nevertheless, when we try to accept these teachings, the mind brings us to the usual impasse. On the one hand, the Masters say this world is of dream-like texture, a passing show, an unreality, a gross distortion by mind and maya (illusion) of the reality that is a state of joy and ecstasy. "Awake," they say, "from this heavy, slothful dream, this nightmare caused by the five distortions of mind. Train the mind, put it in its rightful place as servant not master, and at last give release to your soul."

On the other hand, the mind, sensing an argument, says: "Now do be reasonable. This life is not a dream; it is positive enough. Pinch yourself and see whether or not you are asleep, then get up and have a good time. You are only young once and life is short. You owe it to yourself." And so it goes on with all the old clichés.

If you fall for this "logic," you will once again perpetuate the situation that has kept you so heavily mortgaged with karma. If, instead, you follow the Masters' teaching, you will come to see the role the mind plays in delaying your final destiny. The advice of Sant Mat is this: give the Master your whole attention, and he will show you the door to the kingdom of heaven and how to open it. Thereafter, you may rely upon his presence for guidance all the way to Sach Khand.

Again the mind, still not to be outdone, retorts impatiently: "I have heard all this before, but where is this door, this kingdom of heaven within? The anatomist has never discovered any sign of it. It is illogical; it cannot be proven!" It also argues with a sly touch. "Even if it were possible, you can see for yourself that it is the way of a selfish man; the truly unselfish person must stay to help his fellow men."

But let us postulate a case: a child born in a slum or in degrading circumstances takes for granted his home and surroundings because, for the moment, he knows no other. But there comes at some time a growing doubt in his mind as to the rightness of his conditions. His first impulse may be to run away, but it is more likely that he will remain with his parents for a while, frustrated and bewildered though he may be. As the years pass, there comes the urge to change the conditions that keep his people so downtrodden. But since he has no training in social reform, one could imagine the results of his efforts. They would end like the efforts of a young disciple of a guru, who, stirred by compassion, rescued a lamb from a bird of prey. With some sense of self-righteousness, he related the incident to his Master. The guru, to his surprise, thoughtfully nodded his head but said, "Now think for a while! Do you realize that the bird had not had a meal for several days and was starving?"

Since our would-be reformer cannot wipe out the poor conditions in which he lives, the only reasonable thing for him to do is to withdraw from them. This is the course we are implored to take by all the saints and Masters. This solution is a simple and practical one. Since we cannot alter the world to fit our circumscribed ideas of fitness, we can change our own position in regard to it. Making the effort in the right conditions, raising the attention under the Master's guidance, as we have described, progressively enlightens one on the purpose of human existence. That purpose is to gain release from this bondage and suffering.

To say that these efforts are selfish is as foolish as saying that one must not go to a university (even as the result of his own diligence) until *all* can go to a university, or that one must not accept promotion until *all* can be similarly promoted. Is it selfish to learn to swim before attempting the rescue of drowning men?

Arguments aside, the saints say that so much of this is beyond our present range of vision or understanding. Why not take the trouble to go inside and see for ourselves? The Master gives the technique at initiation and promises that, if it is followed sedulously, it invariably brings results.

17

THE TENTH DOOR

The Masters liken the human body to a house with ten doors. The lower nine of them—the eyes, ears, nostrils, mouth and lower apertures—lead outwards to the material world. The tenth door—situated above and behind the eyes in the hypothalamus, close to the pineal gland—is the only one that leads inwards and upwards, and its presence is almost unknown.

Although this door is mentioned so often in so many religions and philosophies as something that must be reached, opened and passed through, its practical significance and vital importance are unrecognized by all except saints and mystics. They tell us that it is the only door to the higher states of consciousness. Its closing is tragic, as our predicament shows. Its opening is the true beginning of spiritual awareness.

When the prophets of old were said to have journeyed to "a high place" for meditation or consultation with God, they were not going up onto a mountain or hillock. The door in the forehead was the high place where, in the silence of meditation, they transferred their attention to the higher consciousness.

Masonry makes reference to this same point when it describes the middle of the temple where the master consciousness was slain by the five rebellious apprentices, who foolishly desired to obtain the secrets of the inner life before they qualified for them.

So the genuine secrets were lost when the consciousness was separated from God. And the door was closed only to be opened again by a living Master at the proper moment. But we demonstrate once again that somewhere in our consciousness lies the knowledge of this mysterious door, for when we are in desperate straits we dramatically cry "My God," and the hand flies to the forehead.

This fateful door is called by innumerable names in many tongues—the *tisra til*, the third eye, the eye of Siva, the eye above that sees all, the eye of the needle, the wicket gate, and so on. Beyond it lies the path, the Tao, the way; and beyond it lie the happiness and sanity we seek.

But how do we find this door? Omar Khayyám, the Persian mystic, did not find it in the company of his learned friends, for he says:

> Myself when young did eagerly frequent
> Doctor and Saint, and heard great argument
> About it and about: but evermore
> Came out by the same door where in I went.
>
> *The Rubáiyát of Omar Khayyám*

Passing through the third eye or tenth door is only possible with the proper technique of silence, concentration and meditation. It cannot be found through learned argument, which is like several people struggling for the possession of a valuable mirror. In the heat of argument, it is dropped and broken into a thousand splinters. Each splinter gives but a tiny glimpse of reality.

The act of passing through the tenth door is not

to be confused with physical death, although the only difference is that, with willful passage, the soul remains connected to the body, whereas, at the time of death, the connection is severed. It is, on the contrary, an act of life, of being born into a higher state of consciousness. This experience is not a solitary phenomenon as is physical death, but something that can be repeated infinitely. As Professor Puri explains in *Mysticism, the Spiritual Path*, "This is mystic dying, and mystics can go into subtle worlds hundreds of times during the day."

We can now understand the cryptic phrase of St. Paul, "I die daily," and of Guru Nanak, "Such a mystic practice dost thou follow, O Nanak, that thou diest even while living." This paradox of dying while living is behind the saints' message to the world that death can be overcome. But as we know, the way to overcome death has remained a mystery except to mystics.

The ability to pass through the tenth door at will cannot be attained without long practice and great devotion. Once entrance is gained, the disciple ascends through the regions of many mansions, which are very fairly described in Sant Mat books such as *Path of the Masters* and *With a Great Master in India*, by Julian Johnson, *Mysticism, the Spiritual Path*, by L. R. Puri, and *Sar Bachan* by Swami Ji.

These descriptions disprove what many people say, that no one has ever come back from the "other worlds" to tell us about them. They have always been known to the Masters and their advanced disciples, but during the many periods of religious intolerance and bitter theological schisms, it was well-nigh impossible to broach the subject. Those who did so were almost invariably the victims of persecution and even death for heresy. Their teachings were willfully suppressed or distorted, and from this arose the morass of religious bewilderment and doubt.

The possibility of passing, in life, from one state of consciousness to another has been the import of all the great messages to the world from the saints. Their perpetual teaching is that this little planet earth, which so preoccupies us, is but a drop in the ocean of existence available to man, and that the mystic death of entering the tenth door is only a shifting of the scenery for another and far greater episode in the story.

This larger vision has always been beyond the understanding of most. But the concept of other planes of existence may be somewhat easier to grasp for the twentieth century mind, which has expanded the old narrow concepts of matter. From the infinite realms of astrophysics to the invisible energy bundles of elementary particle physics, we are pushing back the laws to which we understand the physical world to conform. And what then? From physics to metaphysics is not far.

How do we know that the things we are taught in our childhood are true? And however much we may trust and admire our teachers, could it not be that some of them may not be so very certain of their own steps? Sant Mat does not ask for such blind belief. The Masters do not ask anyone to accept them or their teachings without question. Instead they invite one to put them to the test, to go in and see for one's self. In Sant Mat, quite literally, seeing is believing.

For this experience, great learning or erudition is not necessary; indeed, thoughts of any kind are a bar. In the words of Jakob Boehme, from *Dialogues on the Supersensual Life*, "It is in thee, and if thou canst my son, for awhile cease from all thinking and willing, then thou shalt hear the unspeakable words of God." All of the great ones have insisted upon simplicity and have abjured both complexity and sophistication. And it goes without saying that these transcendental moments are jewels that neither wealth of words nor riches can buy.

It seems that people often regard religion as something of social value; something to be taken out of the cupboard, dusted off and displayed on holy days, then put away again for the rest of the week; something apart from their daily lives. But to be of most value, our search for God should continue every minute of every day.

Daily meditative practice imparts an indescribable quality, an aroma, an awareness that pervades every action. It is not an intellectual change, but rather a change in sensitivity that could be likened to the development of photography. When the wonders of photography were introduced, the sensitized plate on which the image was recorded required long exposure to produce a picture. The process was quite laborious. But research and development have so increased the sensitivity of the emulsion, and therefore the fineness of the image, that the applications and possibilities of photography, such as microphotography, seem limitless.

The analogy must be clear. It is the increase in

sensitivity and receptivity of the soul, the change from coarse to fine perception developed by the spiritual research called meditation, that makes it possible for the soul to pass through the tenth door to the limitless realms of the higher planes. The more effective the meditation the greater the sensitization of the soul and the higher it can go.

Spiritual practice has further parallels in photography. When taking a picture, one focuses the camera lens, then trips the shutter to let the light hit the film. In meditation, one focuses the attention so that the inner eye can open and the soul can receive the light of the upper regions. But to develop these revelations, the soul, like the photographer, needs a darkroom. For this, any quiet and secluded spot where one can contemplate in silence will serve.

To pursue the analogy still further: in photography, amateur experience produces amateurish results. The same in meditation. So it is wise to avoid the seductive pitfalls of the mind by undertaking meditation only under the guidance of a living Master, a saint in the true sense of the word, a realized soul, a Satguru. Only this brings about true spiritual communion.

18

DIET AND KARMA

Sant Mat is sometimes referred to as Surat Shabd Yoga, but it is not allied to the more widely known schools of yoga. It does not rely upon bodily positions (*asanas*) nor upon breath control (*pranayama*). *Surat* means soul, *shabd* means the Word or Sound Current, and *yoga* means union. Sant Mat, therefore, is the spiritual practice of meditation or concentration that unites the soul with the Word, which is God. This meditation, under the guidance of a true saint, takes the soul on its journey—in this life and after death—to inner and more enlightened regions of peace, serenity and love.

Sant Mat does not require asceticism, but at the same time, it is most definite upon the matter of detachment from everything that retards the progress of the soul. Indeed, the Masters say progress is impossible for one still beset with passions and material desires. The attention must be removed from the nine outer doors and applied undivided to the tenth door and the new objective beyond. Nothing should be done to handicap the training of the mind upwards.

We are all familiar with Christ's teaching that wealth is a hindrance to spiritual progress: "It is easier for a camel to go through the eye of a needle than for a rich man to enter the kingdom of God." And as

Guru Nanak says, "The favoured of Mammon, of soul so dull, such ones can never be attuned to the heavenly Harmony."

The reason for this is simple. As they say in the East, he who has cows, has care of cows. That is, someone with wealth must spend his time looking after it. This creates a vicious cycle, for the more something dominates our thoughts, the more attached we become to it and the more of it we want. Maharaj Sawan Singh says, "Worldly riches attract many people to the extent they are dominated by worldly attachments and cannot hear the Divine Music within." For the journey inwards and upwards, material considerations are entirely left behind because, in the inner regions, they have no value at all.

It is obviously a difficult *volte-face* for a person used to building and guarding worldly treasures or power to become humble and start again at a different level. But if one has taken the effort to search for a living Guru and has finally found one, it is reasonable to carry out his instructions to the fullest. These instructions include continuing with one's work to avoid being a burden upon others, avoiding cruelty in all forms and keeping the body in good health as far as possible.

These last two instructions point up a lesser known (at least to Westerners) hindrance to spiritual progress: improper diet. The Masters insist upon a diet that does not incur the heavy karma of killing:

> I never gave permission to anyone to eat meat in my life. A mother does not administer poison to her own children. In R.S. [Radha Soami] Faith animal food cannot be allowed under any conditions.

> It hardens the heart, and makes the soul dull and heavy.
>
> *Spiritual Gems,*
> Maharaj Sawan Singh

Every time there is a reference to diet and karma, those fateful words of Maharaj Charan Singh leap to the mind of a disciple:

> And the goats, cattle, fowl, etc., how they are mercilessly slaughtered to fill our bellies. Do we ever think how we would feel if we were to change places with them and suffer similar tortures? Let us not forget that the Law of Karma is inexorable and we will have to reap what we have sown.
>
> *Light on Sant Mat*

These words remind the author of an incident that occurred when he accompanied the present Master on a short journey in his car in India. The party had reached a place where the Master was going to consult someone about canal irrigation. We stopped at a bridge over a small river with a sluice gate, over which a moderate force of water was flowing. On the lower side, in shallow water, was a strange sight. The river was almost solid with fish. Men waded in with baskets again and again, filling them each time and emptying them onto sacks lying on the bank.

For a moment the Master regarded this wriggling mass of desperate things, but he quickly turned away with a sigh and with a great depth of feeling said, "A most distressing sight." He left an impression—indeed a conviction in one's soul—that he saw not just a simple harvesting of fish, but the cruel ravages of karma on the souls trapped in those writhing bodies. Looking back on the incident, one could not help seeing a close parallel to the human whirlpool.

We are always told that our great religious teachers were perfected men to be emulated in every possible way. Can any sincere follower of Christ, the Buddha or any other exemplar of love imagine any one of them cutting a throat or wringing a neck in order to enjoy the luxury of a feast? It is a shocking thought.[1]

It is significant that the great Masters will only give discipleship to those who are prepared to undertake the physical and karmic cleansing of the diet they prescribe. This diet includes complete abstinence from flesh foods—be they fish, fowl or animal—eggs, alcohol and anything containing them in any form. Milk, butter, cheese, yoghurt, cream and other milk derivatives are allowed, but neither a slaughtered animal nor any of its post-mortem products may be eaten.

There is no compromise with the general principles of this strict regime, even when medical or physiological reasons are advanced against it, for as the Masters say, there is plenty of choice among necessary and even luxury foods that are purely vegetarian and fruitarian.

> It should be possible for you to arrange a good vegetarian menu which would supply all the necessary elements of nourishment, including especially the proteins, and at the same time be helpful to your liver. "Plenty of raw liver," as the doctors gratuitously advised you, would, in India, be considered a beastly

[1]It is not generally known that Jesus and his brothers were Essenes, a traditionally vegetarian sect.

> suggestion by most people . . . Those who wish to follow a spiritual course know the disadvantage and easily discard injurious habits and foods. You might be interested to know that even Mohammedans, who are habitually a meat-eating people, abstain from flesh diet completely when they follow an intensive spiritual course.
>
> It is our own karmas that are worked out on our bodies in the form of ill health or disease and it would not be in our better and ultimate interest to adopt wrong methods and wrong foods. I appreciate your sincerity and your devotion in seeking advice, and your anxiety to do the right thing; but I regret that it is not possible for me to make a compromise upon this point and advise you contrary to the principles of Sant Mat. Love and devotion can do much more than people sometimes think.
>
> *Light on Sant Mat,*
> Maharaj Charan Singh

It may at first be thought by some that the standards of conduct and diet of Sant Mat are difficult to achieve and arbitrary in nature. But the Masters tell us that attempting to rid the mind of worldly desires while still eating flesh or drinking alcohol is like trying to put out a fire with petrol. The physical and mental actions are so intertwined that the simple matter of diet can help us to control the five perversions of mind—lust, anger, greed, attachment and egotism—and all the psychological ill effects that accompany them.

There may be some preliminary difficulties with the diet, but considering the nature of the objective, one must expect to make reasonable adjustments in one's regimen. This is being done quite well by people in all walks of life including military service.

After a short trial, one will find that the diet is accompanied by many pleasant advantages. There is a gratifying freshness about it.

It should be very clear by now that the one purpose of every instruction given in Sant Mat is to help the disciple reach the *tisra til* or third eye, behind the forehead. His ability to perceive true reality, to understand the eternal verities and, indeed, to attain spiritual salvation depends upon his reaching that door. Therefore, any action—mental or physical—that keeps his perception of that door obscured is wrong and to be studiously avoided.

It has already been pointed out that Sant Mat considers the human body to be a most precious gift and a high attainment in evolution. Its only purpose is to serve the soul as the vehicle for the return home. Therefore, it must be maintained in as efficient a condition as possible for whatever span of time is ordained for this life. Both undernourishment and overeating are spiritual deterrents, but each individual must find his own balance in between. Anyone who does not, is likely to be further proof of the saying that we live on one-third of what we eat, while the doctors live on the other two-thirds.

Many people who have not experienced a vegetarian diet seem to think that it must lead to undernourishment. But they either forget or do not realize that many millions of humans live that way quite apart from any special philosophy. As for physical strength and fitness, it is worth a reminder that the strongest and often the most useful animals—such as the cow, the horse, the sheep, the buffalo and the elephant—find their strength and stamina through grains, grasses and other vegetable products. Athletic prowess is not in any way curtailed by not eating meat; many vegetarian athletes can claim records in their sports.

The old arguments based upon anthropological evidence, such as comparative dental anatomy, as being proof of man's need for a mixed diet, do not concern us here. We are presumably aiming to transcend the status of human animal to become, by the grace of Satguru, something more.

It only requires some slight conviction and a short trial to be entranced by, amongst other things, the sense of cleanliness and well-being and of the fitness in the scheme of things of a vegetarian diet. The seeker who wishes to try such a diet can explore a new and interesting range of menus of infinite variety. This should finally rule out any feelings of sacrifice or deprivation.

Since this chapter is not intended to be a rhapsody of dietary excellence other than as it influences spiritual practice, some attention should be given to the deeper and more important considerations of the diet; i.e., the human relationship to the lower species over which man was, according to the book of Genesis, given dominion. According to Indian teachings, there are eighty-four *lakh* (8,400,000) species belonging to five kingdoms or groups—vegetable, insect, bird, animal and human. Together they form the line of evolution and devolution, of reincarnation and transmigration, called *chaurasi*, the wheel of eighty-four.

We are taught that the differences among the five groups are due to five attributes, known as *tattwas*.

These attributes are in everything in the universe, but they are not active in the five groups in the same proportions. Humans are unique in that all of the five attributes are active in them, and only in them is the fifth and highest attribute, *akash* (ether), active. *Akash* is the attribute of discrimination and is the one thing that differentiates humans from animals, enabling them to achieve self-realization and immortality. They must not neglect or squander it.

Since we have all the attributes in common with the lower species,[1] even if, in them, those attributes are lying dormant, it is certainly pertinent to ask if they have souls. The answer is yes, and our religious philosophies insist that God is in everything.

> There is not such an unbridgeable gap between the human and the animal, since we have all the same attributes. The key lies in the *akash*. Encourage the small percentage of *akash* in animals and they become almost human; discourage *akash* in humans, they become subhuman, almost animal.

It is the presence of this one attribute in the human make-up, the faculty of discrimination, that enables man to achieve self-realization, which is the prerequisite of God-consciousness. If full advantage is taken of this faculty and it is nurtured and developed from coarse grain to fine grain, it can lead to all those desirable things of which we have heard and of which we are given glimpses in our inspirational moments, i.e., perfected or spiritual man.

If, on the other hand, this quality is not appreciated, if it is degraded, squandered or lost, we are relegated to subhuman status through transmigration.

---

[1]The Masters point out that the lower species also have wives, brothers and children and that like us they eat, sleep, feel pain and so forth.

We sink back into the wheel of eighty-four *lakh* species. Once a human always a human, is not the teaching of the saints. Lack of compassion, cruelty and abuse have to be paid back at the appropriate level, even though it may be subhuman. We should realize that we can develop onerous karmic ties with animals as well as with our fellow men and that the former are as burdensome to a spiritual life as the latter.

At present, the overwhelming percentage of our life is lived downwards through the nine doors of the physical body, with only a minute proportion devoted upwards to the tenth door. It is beyond dispute that as we think, as we act and as we eat, so we become. If we think coarsely, if we kill to eat or if we act with cruelty, we become gross; and the converse is equally true. Therefore, it is utterly essential to spiritual progress to cultivate an ethical and moral way of life and to eat only the simplest and purest of nourishment.

Of course, it is not possible totally to avoid creating karma when we eat, but we must come as near as possible. Since the vegetable kingdom has only one active *tattwa*, the karma involved in eating this species is very light and can easily be taken care of by meditation. The more active the *tattwas*, the higher the species is in the scale of evolution, and the greater is the responsibility involved in killing it. Hence the great burden of karmas assumed in killing cows, sheep, pigs and the like, and the need for the warning "Thou shalt not kill."

The oft-debated point of the egg being harmless or blameless if it is infertile is beside the point. It still can be classified generically and chemically as dead animal matter and is therefore forbidden by Sant Mat. Its contents are sulphurous and stimulating to those lower human centres, from which we are to withdraw our attention. It aggravates lust and anger, making the ascent to *tisra til* that much more difficult.

Many religions that do not perhaps aim so high, often compromise in dietary matters, especially with alcohol (which reduces the sense of responsibility and scatters the attention) and with eating for pleasure. The follower of a Satguru can make no such compromise of principles because he wants to break, not to add to, the countless fetters of karma that bind him to the earth.

These efforts bring to mind the story of *Gulliver's Travels*, in which the sailor Gulliver was shipwrecked and washed up on a strange coast in the land of Lilliput. He awakened slowly to consciousness to find himself lying tightly tethered by a thousand tiny ropes that were pegged to the earth. He could scarcely move a finger for the bonds, but gradually, as he exerted his strength, the tiny ligatures gave way one by one, releasing him sufficiently to take stock of his new and strange position among the little Lilliputians. His eventual freedom liberated him into a new world.

Our worldly bonds are like Gulliver's ties. They appear so tiny, yet together they are so terribly strong. Most of them are the result of the five perversions of mind. But through the practice of Nam *bhakti*—that is, listening to the creative Sound Current in meditation—the disciples of Sant Mat progressively sever all the thousands of ties of bondage, bringing about, little by little, true detachment and the liberation of the soul into higher realms. They eventually become saints among men.

Maharaj Jagat Singh used another metaphor for describing how we must detach the soul from the world. He said that the soul is so enslaved in the activities of the mind and emotions that it is like a shawl caught up in a thorny bush. The shawl must be removed thorn by thorn to prevent tearing the cloth. Only one who, like the author himself, has experienced this desperate and exasperating situation of being caught upon an Indian thorn hedge can truly appreciate the predicament. It seems that for each thorn freed, two more are caught up. To remove the cloth roughly, without supreme care and infinite patience, would ruin it with holes.

So the detachment of the soul, thorn by thorn, from the tangle of karma without harming it is the loving service of the Satguru. If the disciple does not follow his Master's advice and instructions, he will continue to suffer through his fate. But he has the means by which to leave the pain of worldly thorns behind.

> You know that all of us have to work out our pralabdh karmas. The law is inexorable; but by the practice of Nam and Shabd we are enabled to rise above the sufferings, and to face the situation with confidence and ease. The more we practise Simran and Shabd, the more we rise above the body, and therefore are indifferent to any suffering to which the body may be subject. The account, however, must be settled by everybody.
>
> *Light on Sant Mat*,
> Maharaj Charan Singh

19

INNER LIGHTS AND SOUNDS

In cultivating the power of inner perception, the adjustment of diet comes first. The second step which the Masters teach, the most difficult of all the stages, is to control the mind. This is accomplished by what is known as simran; that is, the repetition of sacred words over and over again to occupy the wayward mind. Complete instructions in this method are given to the disciple at the time of initiation. Simran gradually calms the emotional turmoil that distracts us daily from spiritual things and enables the mind to concentrate on God.

But to train one's mind to behave as one wishes it to, is a matter of time and infinite patience. It is necessary to remind oneself continually that absorption in the lower physical centres and their activities drags the mind downwards. It obscures our consciousness of, and therefore the functioning of, the higher faculties. And although we are told that an initiate is never lost from the path, no matter how far he may appear to stray, indulgence in the sense pleasures can delay his progress considerably.

To encourage us, the Master tells us that Sant Mat is *comparatively* an easy road. But we still have to recognize that the climb is steep and arduous. Quite long periods of meditation each day, done in a spirit of devotion, are necessary to still the mind. This may take one hour, two hours or even more of repetition.

Once we have stilled the mind and raised the attention to the eye centre, the Sound Current (which at this level is described as a bell or a conch) takes over and begins to pull the soul up like a magnet. This part of meditation is called bhajan, and this listening to Shabd or the Word lifts the consciousness upwards to those places and experiences that are so often spoken of in the many sacred books. Before this stage is reached, however, the disciple still reaps untold benefits from meditation. Even the very earliest efforts are accompanied by subtle changes in values, a new sense of balance and feelings of peace and contentment.

If this sounds somewhat exotic, think of the powerful influence, good or evil, that external music can exert on us. Some popular music can be quite detrimental because it tends to stir up our baser passions, while a choir or an orchestra can unquestionably produce emotional uplift. However, the uplift of the Shabd is infinitely more effective and lasting. It is described as unalloyed happiness or bliss but it is calm and unemotional bliss.

In his youth, the author was occasionally embarrassed by the question asked by evangelists, "Have you seen the light?" meaning "Have you been saved?" "Are you on the path?" "Have you joined our organization?" But it does not now seem so very strange that they should use that particular form of expression, for in all times and in all tongues there has been a continual reference in sacred literature not only to sound but also to light. Any path would be dark indeed without illumination.

Light, as well as sound, is always within us, no matter how deeply it may be buried. The Masters can easily see the kindling light of souls ready for the path of *bhakti*. Thereupon, they draw them to their presence.

The Path of the Masters speaks of the soul, or the newly aroused consciousness, passing through the "gates of light" into a new world. This is another way to describe raising the attention to the third eye and into a higher dimension. And the Bible has this to say about the third eye:

> The light of the body is the eye: if therefore thine eye be single,[1] thy whole body shall be full of light.
>
> But if thine eye be evil, thy whole body shall be full of darkness.
>
> New Testament

Eastern religions speak of *jot* (in Sanskrit) or *jyoti* (in Hindi) as the light of the first heavenly region. This light comes from the luminous petals of a thousand-petalled lotus.

There should be no doubt that these things are realities, and to those who practise the way of Sant Mat, the nature of the lights, like the sounds, is an indication of what stage on the journey has been reached. Descriptions of the sounds and lights can be gathered from all sides. Two may be quoted from the Bible that also have other facets of interest to the students of Sant Mat. Firstly, St. John:

> There was a man...named Nicodemus, a ruler of the Jews:
>
> The same came to Jesus [with questions]...

[1]The attention focused at the third eye by successful meditation.

Jesus answered...Verily, verily, I say unto thee, Except a man be born again, he cannot see the kingdom of God [which is within].

Nicodemus saith...How can a man be born when he is old? Can he enter the second time into his mother's womb, and be born?

Jesus answered...I say unto thee, Except a man be born of water and of the Spirit [the Holy Ghost or Nam], he cannot enter into the kingdom of God [cannot pass through the tenth door]...

Marvel not that I said unto thee, Ye must be born again.

The wind bloweth where it listeth, and thou hearest the sound thereof, but canst not tell whence it cometh, and whither it goeth...[1]

Nicodemus answered...How can these things be?

Jesus...said unto him, Art thou a master in Israel, and knowest not these things?

It seems that the Sound Current, the heavenly Bani in its many forms, was completely unknown to Nicodemus, although he was acting as a Master. But there are many who call themselves Masters with very little claim to true inner experience of a high nature.

The second reference comes from Acts:

And suddenly there came a sound from heaven as of a rushing mighty wind, and it filled all the house where they were sitting.

And there appeared unto them cloven tongues... of fire, and sat upon each of them.

And they were filled with the Holy Ghost...

The sound and light described somewhat dramatically here are not unfamiliar to the mystic.

[1]Italics added by author.

The Bani [prayer] that we recite every day is the road and not the destination. It serves our purpose only when it leads to the Anahad Bani [the unstruck sound or the silent music within], which takes us to our real destination.

The rituals of different religions are strikingly similar. In all our temples, mosques, and churches, bells are rung and there are lights on the altar. These are merely symbols of what is encountered in the inner temple. Instead of hearing the sound and seeing the lights inside, we remain prey to our outward tendencies. Saints point out the reality within and induce us to achieve it.

Our mind can contact the true Shabd through the mercy and grace of Satguru. Thus all its coverings of rust and filth are removed, and it shines forth in its own glory. So when it is transformed from dross into gold, it reaches its own true abode [Brahm, Trikuti, or universal mind]. The soul is then free to reach its real home in Sat Desh [true heaven or Sach Khand].

Discourse,
Maharaj Charan Singh

20

PASSING THE DELECTABLE ISLANDS

It is well-nigh impossible to avoid considerable repetition when writing on Sant Mat, for the essential themes weave in and out of each other like the warp and weft of a carpet. So we go back once more to consider the two paths, of knowledge (*gyan*) and of devotion (*bhakti*).

In the search for interesting theories and explanations, the temptation to explore every avenue and leave no stone unturned is great indeed, but the mystic knows full well, often through bitter experience, that the intellectual path is extremely limited in results and strewn with pitfalls. The path of *bhakti* is less concerned with intellectual processes. It is far more direct and efficacious and can be undertaken by the humblest and simplest devotee; it is the putting into practice of intellectual convictions.

The intellectual seeker will perhaps insist upon more precise details of the regions that are so familiar to the saints. The journey is well described up to the second region of Brahm in prolific Oriental literature. But it is the regions beyond Brahm—Parbrahm and Sach Khand—with which Sant Mat is especially concerned.

There is a very concise and useful description of these regions in *Sant Mat and the Bible*, by Narain

Dass. In *The Path of the Masters*, Julian Johnson explains the four grand divisions of nature:

> The entire universe of universes is divided into four grand divisions, each marked out and differentiated from the rest by certain characteristics of the substances composing them, and the nature of the phenomena to be seen there.
>
> (1) Beginning with our own world, and from this point of departure, the first grand division is the physical universe, called in the technical language of the Masters, *Pinda*. It is composed chiefly of matter of varying density, coarse in quality, but mixed with a small percentage of mental and spiritual substances, just enough to give it life and motion...
>
> (2) ... the grand division just above the physical universe is *Anda*.... The substance of Anda is much finer in the structure of its atoms, in its vibratory activity and its degree of density.... Anda is also much more vast in extent than the physical universe.
>
> (3) Next above Anda lies *Brahmanda*, the third grand division.... It is... much more vast in extent. It is also more refined and full of light.... [It] is composed mostly of spirit substance, but is mixed with a refined sort of matter.
>
> (4) ... the highest grand division in all creation [is] the finest and purest, composed entirely of pure spirit. This region is definitely beyond the sphere of matter. There is no mind in this region... Its name is *Sat Desh*.

It is in the many attempts to describe the indescribable, in unsuitable language, to students mostly unfamiliar with the atmosphere and the context or without personal experience, that schools of divergent theologies arise. Analogy and metaphor are, of course, almost universally used, but they are *varnatmak*;[1] that is to say, they are mere symbols. Of themselves they contain no more value than does a medical prescription or a recipe for cooking. The Masters remind one that reading a prescription or recipe over and over or even learning it by heart does not constitute a cure or a meal. It is also no good to debate their merits, going "about it and about" as Omar Khayyám did with "Doctor and Saint." Both have to be put to practical use before any judgement as to their efficacy can be formed.

Since this book is intended to be but an introduction to Sant Mat and to stimulate investigation, it will not attempt to go farther in describing the upper regions. At the early stages it is not necessary and it may be confusing to attempt to learn all the details of the ground to be covered, just as it is not necessary if one is undertaking a considerable terrestrial journey. A fair outline is all that is needed for one to follow the Masters' suggestion: go in and see for yourself and learn as you go.

It is obvious that we must do our learning as apprentices under the guidance of a Master, for it can well be imagined that each region seems, from the one below, to be the highest and our ultimate goal. Naturally, the guide must be one who freely travels this grand path himself and therefore knows it well.

The expression "seventh heaven," used to describe great happiness, implies recognition, however dim, of six other heavens, and these must be passed through safely to reach home. To pass through all

---

[1]The spoken or written word, as compared to *dhunatmak*, the unwritten or silent Word, which supersedes language.

these various heavens or paradises unaided is impossible. Unless we have a firm and knowledgeable guide who can keep our eyes on the goal ahead, we are certain to be enticed from the path by their beguiling splendour and become lost, just as Ulysses would have fallen prey to the song of the Sirens had he not plugged his crew's ears with beeswax and had himself lashed to the mast. Only when we have reached our home in the most beautiful and blissful region of all are we no longer tempted by the lesser beauty below.

On his journey home to Ithaca, Ulysses had to sail past the hazards of many islands, some delectable, some deadly, and endure great trials and temptations. The Guru sees to it that the path of bhakti is a safer one, for the disciple is at all times under his immediate supervision. His responsibility is to take his disciples to their real home in Sach Khand, conducting them through the several heavens safely and avoiding all the seductive side attractions.

Lesser sages revere the exaltedness of universal mind—the Om of the Vedas—and conclude that it is the Absolute. But it is still part of the created world and is thus subject to dissolution. Therefore, Sant Mat regards the region of Brahm, as well as the physical and astral regions, as changeable and illusory. It is not the home of the soul but of Kal or Mammon, the negative power, and of Maya, illusion.

> If any yogi or other man claiming to be a Master teaches that *Brahm Lok* or the region of Brahm is the highest of heavens, and that Brahm is the supreme God, then you may know of a certainty that he is not a Master. For the Brahm Lok is only the second of the higher regions, or planes, while above that are six other planes, in an ascend-

> ing scale, each higher and greater than the one below it. In the Grand Hierarchy of the Universe, Brahm, the ruler of *Trikuti* and the three worlds, is but a subordinate under the Supreme One.
>
> *Path of the Masters*,
> Julian Johnson

We are taught that not until it reaches the region above Brahm has the soul served its apprenticeship in matter and does not have to reincarnate. It is to this high estate that a disciple of a Master should aspire; therefore, he exerts himself to reduce his outstanding karma by using every means of devotion shown to him by the Master.

The worlds of mind and matter, then, in spite of their glories and temptations, are what the soul has to disentangle itself from, if it is to experience and to benefit from its own immortality. Above the realms of mind and matter, only "devotion consciousness" and love can exist. This kind of devotion is not the kind that shows itself as religious fervour or fanaticism; it is far beyond emotion. Without this kind of devotion, all our longing and crying for freedom is an empty gesture.

True *Gurbhakti*, or devotion for the Master, is an accomplishment that, for most disciples, is achieved slowly. What may start as incredulity when a seeker first meets the path changes to intellectual acceptance before he is initiated. Then, through meditation, he gains positive conviction of the teachings, and devotion automatically grows. Meanwhile, many favourite convictions of the past have to be modified or rejected, especially those about the unbridgeable gap between this world and that, between life and death. Since the two are interpenetrating, it is possible by practical experience to replace the fear of the unknown with the joy of anticipation of what lies beyond death.

The moral codes and precepts laid down by great spiritual teachers throughout the ages are simple guides for a rather unruly and unthinking mass of humanity, but the mystical, more advanced instructions that they give to their disciples are different in intention. These instructions are concerned with the inner path, but except by a few, they are rarely accepted and tested and are therefore not understood. They are often greeted with incredulousness, with ridicule and even with anger. Indeed, we all know that Christ was killed for his unorthodox inner doctrines, as were many redeemers of the soul of man.

In spite of the cold and hostile receptions of the past, the saints continue to come to this world to disentangle the soul and reestablish the lines of communication with God. This has always been the *raison d'être* of true saints and Satgurus, and it is the object of Sant Mat and of the Master's efforts on behalf of the disciple. The author, in a moment of great enthusiasm, once said to Maharaj Ji: "Sir, how I wish you would come to England to give your message."

"What message?" he said with a smile.

"Your message of Sant Mat. There would be a landslide!"

But he shook his head and said slowly, "There would not, you know."

But the Master did send the following message in 1957 to those Westerners who were already his disciples:

> The soul and the mind being knotted together, as it were, the soul has perforce to follow the mind and

lend its support and, as a result, has to be born again and again to suffer the consequences of the karmas and the longings of the mind. To escape these dire consequences, the mind must be prevented from going out and running after pleasures. It should be withdrawn gradually and made steady at its centre, known as tisra til or the third eye, so that it may contact the Shabd or the audible life stream and rise above the world of phenomena. This is the only way to get permanent release from this prison house.

Saints and mystics have compared the human body to a house with ten doors. The nine apertures —organs—lead outward and involve us in the world; the tenth leads us within to our true home and brings our wanderings to an end. *The secret of this door is known only to saints and mystics, though it has been referred to in the sacred books of almost every religion.*[1]

The pleasures of the world are not only transient but turn into bitterness and disappointment in course of time. No situation here is free from pain and grief. Disease, poverty, disharmony in the family, national jealousies and wars are the lot of man here and make him miserable and wretched. We are kept bound to this world by our karmas, both good and bad, which keep our nose to the grindstone. The karmas that we perform lead to other karmas, which fetter our life and our existence both now as well as in subsequent births.

Saints, therefore, exhort us to turn within, knock at this tenth door and attach ourselves to Shabd, where alone we can find permanent peace and unalloyed happiness. But our desires and attachments stand in the way. Our egoism and desire for possession make us return to this world again and again. Egoism makes us claim and appropriate everything,

[1]Italics added by author.

and the result is that, instead of possessing those things which we want to own, we are possessed by them. We become the slaves of those things, and to such an extent that they occupy our minds even at the time of death; and, according to the well-known rule, we are born again in the surroundings which had so fascinated us. The saints take us out of this difficulty by teaching us Nam Bhakti [devotion to Nam], and thus turn inward and Godward the tides which are now flowing outward.

It is the nature of the mind to run after pleasures, but no pleasure in the world has the power to captivate it forever, and it flits from one subject to another. When, however, it takes to Nam Bhakti and, going in, tastes the bliss of Shabd, its fickleness goes and it becomes steady.

Gurbhakti and Nam Bhakti are the means by which the mind is weaned from sensual pleasures and attached to the Shabd or the audible life stream, which ultimately takes us back to our origin, God.

21

SAINTS ARE MEN OF GOD

The soul is an eagle that has inherited the freedom of the skies but must endure captivity in a cage. That is how the Masters regard this mortal existence, as a cage into which our karmas have brought us again and again. Karmas incurred on this plane have to be worked out on this plane, so we must return to this planet either to give or to receive in kind.

Karmas are not easily understood; they are responsibilities of all kinds, good and bad. They are not necessarily debits; they may also be credits. For instance, a borrower has to pay back what he owes, but the lender has to be present to receive his just dues; the transaction is binding on both sides. Whether the links of karma are of gold or iron depends on the actions and motives of both borrower and lender: Did the borrower obtain the money by fair means and on fair terms? Was the lender a benefactor or guilty of usury? And so on.

Karmas have a habit of growing from small beginnings like a rolling snowball. For instance, a schoolboy bumps another boy—by accident or design. The other boy objects and returns the buffet, but a little harder. So back and forth it goes with emotions increasing until the matter grows all out of proportion. Friends of the two boys may be caught up in the fight, so that the karmas created by the event spread to other lives. When the fight is finally broken up by a teacher, anger, resentment, fear and longing for revenge have made a bond that will bring the boys together again—whether in this life or some future life—to settle the account. During the process of settling the account, more animosity, and therefore more karma, is likely to develop. Thus are worldly relationships perpetuated ad infinitum. Such vast tangles of tragic action made the poet Robert Burns lament:

> Man's inhumanity to man
> Makes countless thousands mourn!

The answer to eliminating the earthly embarrassments and pains of karma is detachment. When we become immune to the desires of mind and the tugs of emotion, our actions can become karmaless. If one of the schoolboys had taken, when the jostling began, the simple step of turning the other cheek or giving a soft answer, he could have obviated the whole catastrophe and would have altered the flow of energy from a downward destructive course through the nine doors to an upward course towards the tenth door of tranquillity and strength. Such conduct requires what may be viewed as superhuman effort, but we are presumably aiming at superhuman status in the end. This book is but a gentle reminder that we are on the threshold—over which anyone may go—of attaining that status.

It is indeed a complicated business, this working out of debit and credit, of cause and effect, of action and reaction. In the physical world, a businessman needs an accountant to keep his bookkeeping straight.

So in the lofty realms of the inner life, it is even more necessary to have someone who is qualified to handle our karmic accounts. We clearly need detached advice, for our own judgement is distinctly unreliable. We need the supreme guidance of one who knows, i.e., a living Master.

The present Master at Beas, Maharaj Charan Singh, in his message to overseas disciples in 1957, explained the purpose of all living Masters:

> On this New Year's Day I have no special message to give but to remind you of the teaching of Maharaj Ji,[1] which he impressed on us all through his life and which constitutes the essence of the teachings of the saints of all times. What is their mission in this world? Saints are men of God, who come here on a mission of mercy to lead the suffering humanity back to the feet of God. That is their only mission in life. They come not to divide but to unite and are above the narrow distinctions of caste or creed. They do not wish to create new sects or castes, though when they pass away, their followers lose sight of their real teachings and take to various types of ritualism and narrow down the teachings, meant for the whole humanity, to particular sects and schools. This gives rise to castes or creeds and even bigotry and fanaticism; but there are no such differences in saints.
>
> Saints of all ages and countries have the same message to give, the same truth to teach. They tell us that the soul is a spark of the divine flame, but its light here is dimmed by mind and maya. They teach us how to pierce these veils and get united again to our source or origin.

As the Master points out, the narrowing down of

[1]His own Guru, Maharaj Sawan Singh Ji.

the original teachings into bigotry and fanaticism kills both their inspiration and their direct inner revelation. The seeker is lost in the host of cross-currents and doubts that have arisen from different interpretations of the same written authority. These interpretations are often inaccurate, distorted and even deliberately falsified. Words, thoughts and meanings are put into the mouths of the original teachers. The pity of it for most of us is that they are not here to confirm what they actually did say.

The advantage of Sant Mat is that one can ask his questions of the Master directly. Further, the disciple can verify his teachings beyond a doubt by firsthand experience; that is, he can go within under the Master's guidance and see for himself, and without having to undertake the difficult practices of the well-known yogas. Surely this statement is both challenging and convincing.

When the Master refers to the process of going in, he speaks of dying daily to worldly things, to paraphrase St. Paul. But this "dying" clearly means attaining to states of higher consciousness without shuffling off this mortal coil.

We are assured that the barriers between us and these higher states of consciousness are by no means insuperable.

> Every human being is capable of experiencing Mystic Transport. This capacity or faculty is present in all men, although in most it remains in a latent or dormant condition all their life...Mysticism is beyond the sphere of Psychology, because it transcends the fundamental duality of subject and object... Mystic Transport...is not imagination,

for imagination is only an analytico-synthetic process of the mind.

Mysticism, the Spiritual Path,
L. R. Puri

The great teachers instruct us in gaining our own immortality, first by "the acquisition of the secret of Nam. Then, by constant application and unceasing devotion, comes the actual realization of Nam." They extend their help and infinite comfort even to the transgressor:

> Even though the seeker may still be steeped in lust and anger, not only is he accepted by the Master, but he is completely refashioned after Him. With His infinite grace, He bestows upon him the gift of Nam, practising which he becomes pure and ultimately reaches his Divine Home. It is for these reasons that he becomes filled with love and devotion for the Master's form and becomes His true lover, with the result that standing, sitting, walking, awake or asleep, he constantly thinks of Him. This, in fact, is the true way to break the spell of duality and unfold the glory of the one Absolute.

Discourses on Sant Mat,
Maharaj Sawan Singh

22

THE SMILES OF TINY CHILDREN

When we see the smiles of tiny children, it is easy to regard them as innocents. But a baby is not born with a clean slate. He comes into this world with the onus of past actions still upon him, his account on this plane still unsettled. His soul, which is eternal, cannot be new, but he receives a new body—the apparatus for earthly existence—that is tailored to fit. His body, together with his heredity and environment, is precisely suited to carry out the fate allotted to this incarnation by the lord of karma.

A newborn is like a cheque that has been written but not yet endorsed. Or as mystics sometimes say, his fate is in his brow. Only this fate can explain why some are born as geniuses or princes while other poor unfortunates are born with the greatest disadvantages.

Almost from the first breath, infants begin to demonstrate a distinct individuality, showing the strongest character trends even in the bud. These variations of character are part of their heritage—their stars. They are the result of karmas accumulated over the long ages, providing such infinite variety that no two people are alike.

The traits and tendencies carried over from past lives (*sanskaras*) may also come in the form of subconscious memories, giving one the impression that he has been somewhere, done something or met someone before—a feeling of instant recognition. Few of us are aware of how much we actually do know because it is so deeply ingrained in us. We occasionally reach some of this subconscious knowledge in times of deep emotion or inspiration, but we can only realize it fully through mystic transport, or going within.

To accomplish mystic transport we must, as has been said, shun the lower nine doors, which give expression to the lower desires, and gain access to the tenth door by cultivating the one *tattwa* that distinguishes us from the lower species—discrimination, or self-awareness. So long as we do not use this tenth door to gain self-awareness and freedom, we remain irrevocably chained to the world of Nature, to the mills of God, which grind exceeding small, and to the harsh life of tooth and claw. We go around and around the wheel of life, with history repeating itself like the days and the seasons.

To those who are as yet content to remain with this world of nature, life after life, there is no particular incentive to seek this most precious tenth door. But to others, this door offers the eternal life that they long for. It is the verification of Christ's teaching that death can be conquered in life. In the words of the Adi Granth: "Every day do I die, and every day do I come back to life: such is the method that my Guru hath taught me."

The verification offered by mystic teachings is that of firsthand experience. As L. R. Puri says:

> Mysticism does not dictate like Philosophy or Religion; it only opens our inner eye so that we may see for ourselves; it only gives us "Light" by which

> we may perceive things in their true colour; it only awakens our transcendent power of perceiving the deep reality of things, and then leaves us to form our own judgment by a firsthand knowledge . . . .
>
> In mysticism we are not required to take things for granted or remain content with mere theoretical understanding. An intellectual grasp of the salient points may help us in doing the mystic practice properly and successfully; but the real object of all mystic training is to have practical realisation of transcendental Truth.
>
> *Mysticism, The Spiritual Path*

And as Tulsi Sahib, a poet-saint of India, said: "When with my own eyes do I behold, then shall I accept what the Satguru saith."

To take a journey, it is not sufficient to read any number of guide books, nor to enquire of travel agencies nor even to book a seat. One has to get going. So for the spiritual journey, it is not advisable to wait until death. It is in the prime of life that this thing should be done, for it requires courage and persistent application of a practical technique. Nevertheless, it is never too late, no matter how old one may be, to begin the search for self-realization, to follow all the clues and admonitions that come to one's searching mind and patiently coordinate all the pieces of life into a coherent philosophy.

One must regard this life as only one episode in a long saga. One's present situation, whether it be at the dizzy heights of success or the depths of despondency, should be regarded as part of a continuum in which one has played both hero and villain, swayed by his own wishes and desires. In this continuum, no effort to realize our true heritage and to reunite with

God is ever lost, even if a whole lifetime is spent in the search. These efforts only increase our desire for God, which is what will eventually take us home. To repeat the words of Maharaj Charan Singh: "Once started on the Path, we go on at our own pace according to our zeal and fervour for God-realization, and the debts of karma which we still have to discharge."

23

THE SOAP OF POVERTY

The final summing up of our circumstances and how Sant Mat can alter them is appropriate.

1. At the creation our spirit emanated from our Father's home. All religions tell us that we are sparks of the Divine Flame, or sons of God.
2. To express itself on the mental and material planes, the soul took on a mental body (mind) and then a physical body. Through these bodies, it became involved in worldly affairs and created karmas that, in turn, created its future fate.
3. It could not now detach itself from the world because of a balance of unpaid karma, so it entered upon an endless chain of cause and effect, or reincarnation and transmigration around the wheel of births and deaths (*chaurasi*). Over a series of incarnations, the mind, becoming fond of the pleasures of the material world, gradually usurped the soul's position of eminence. Through further incarnations its pleasure-seeking became an instinctive, habitual pattern of behaviour that is now difficult to change.

4. At some time the soul cries desperately for help and enlightenment.
5. When the pupil is ready, the Master appears.
6. The Master trains the pupil for the path, the way of self-knowledge, of realization and of final release.
7. The pupil is said to be reborn and has then to practise a life of new values built on the eternal verities.
8. The disciple is no longer concerned with receiving what is due to him. He is now preoccupied with voluntarily redressing his wrongdoings, with affirming his responsibilities and with confessing his faults. (Father, I have sinned and am no more worthy to be called thy son.)
9. Sant Mat is also called Surat Shabd Yoga, or the yoga of the Sound Current. Through meditation and self-discipline, it is designed to change the main flow of our attention from a downward and outward direction through the nine doors of material life, upward to the tenth door. Following the infallible radar of the eternal, audible Sound Current—also known as the Word, Logos, Shabd, Tao and Bani, to name a few—the disciple passes through this door to the various heavens, including Brahmand (universal mind), and finally to Sach Khand, our true Home.

In Brahmand, the disciple experiences an exalted state of consciousness that the Buddhists call Nirvana. In the West this is often wrongly thought to be a state of nothingness or a kind of blackout, but in reality it is a state of "everythingness."

> For when thou enterest that Door, beyond both pleasure and pain dost thou go.
>
> Maulana Rum

However, even this state of bliss is not the highest but is a stepping stone. The final freedom is the indescribable ideal, which is nevertheless described variously as Oneness, absolute and utter surrender, merging with the Ocean, or uniting with the Beloved. The Masters teach that this freedom can be attained while in the human form, but only under the guidance of a living Master.

10. The Master or saint or Satguru, who is no ordinary man, takes some of the disciple's burden of karma upon himself and helps the disciple to pay off the rest. *Pralabdh* or fate karma, the karma allotted for this life, must be gone through. Creating new karma must be avoided by strict adherence to the Master's instructions on diet and moral living. *Sinchit* karma, the huge store of accumulated karma waiting for future lives, is transmuted by *Gurbhakti*, devotion to the Guru. If this cannot be accomplished in one lifetime, the disciple is given another birth in surroundings more suited to spiritual discipline. Maharaj Sawan Singh says:

> In Sant Mat philosophy the sins and shortcomings are viewed by the Master in the same light as a washerman regards the dirt on a cloth. He cares for the cloth and not

the least for the dirt. His aim is to cleanse the cloth by some means or other; whether by the gentle method of applying soap or by the rough and ready method of beating the cloth against a slab of stone. It depends upon his will.

In the same way the Master aims at reforming his disciples and curing them of their bad habits and wicked deeds so that the spirit may shine in its purity. He determines as to life's procedure. At first he points out our mistakes in gentleness and with love. If this fails, then he adopts a less gentle course and if even that does not serve its purpose, then he applies drastic remedies. In short, he is bent on reforming.

To explain the matter more fully, the Master at first tries to purify us by his discourses. If this fails, then he applies the soap of poverty, adversity and disease. If these do not answer the purpose, then he gives another birth to the disciple. He does not rest until he has taken the spirit of his disciple to its Source. Even if the pupil deserts him, becomes hostile towards him or wishes to injure him, he does not slacken his efforts.

Spiritual Gems

11. There are many influences at work to prevent or retard the attainment of the ideals that are taught by saints and messiahs of all time, but the greatest difficulty of them all is the mind, for it is the instrument of the negative power and has its own vested interests and preoccupations in the transient, evanescent material regions.

The five perversions of the untrained mind—lust, anger, greed, attachment and egotism—are the great fomenters of trouble. They spin the insidious web of karma that binds us hand and foot. As the mind is slowly brought to heel, cleaned and purified by the Satguru, who as he himself says is the washerman, it will begin to serve its true purpose. The nearer it is brought to the realm of universal mind, the less it is distracted by worldly temptations and the purer it becomes. It gives way as master of the soul to become its servant, freeing the soul to continue its journey unencumbered.

12. The soul is not allowed to re-enter its home in Sach Khand until it has discharged all of its karmic debts; hence, the length and arduousness of the spiritual journey. Imagine the predicament that would arise if a soul was able to enter prematurely, still harbouring earthly longings and desires. A restless heaven would be not far removed from hell.

24

THE ONE GOD OF US ALL

Out of Nam, out of the breath of Brahm, out of the Word was everything made that was made. But the manifestation of the objective, three-dimensional world of the physical plane, when compared with the dynamic, infinite Source, is but the flash of a pocket torch against the light of a million suns. That is why saints call this world negative and ephemeral and warn us not to regard it as real or important.

In the physical world, living forms are like pieces of pottery. Obviously, they are useful and necessary if the soul must exist here. But consciousness or life itself does not depend upon these objects. They are external shells that can be changed or broken or disintegrated by time, leaving only a few mournful remains for the archaeologist. They are made of matter that "moth and rust doth corrupt," and they are ruled by cycles.[1] A true mystic is concerned only with being released from the forms and cycles that imprison his soul.

> Saints of all ages and countries have the same message to give, the same Truth to teach. They tell us that the soul is a spark of the Divine Flame,

---

[1]Physical cycles such as tides, time cycles such as days and seasons and the cycle of both time and matter—the wheel of birth and death.

> but its light here has been dimmed by Mind and Maya. They teach us how to pierce these veils and get united again to our Source or Origin.
>
> People give Him different names, according to their liking, but He who is known by all these [names] is One without a second. They call Him Ram, Allah, Vah-i-Guru, Radhaswami or God; but He is one and the same. He is the one God of us all. There are no differences or limitations of caste, creed, color or country for Him. He alone is eternal and for all times and ages. He alone is eternal, permanent; all else is mortal, transient. In the beginning—before time—He alone was and created the whole universe out of Nam, which is also called the Word, Logos or Shabd. Man is the epitome of the universe and is also the real Temple of God, where He can be realized. It is for teaching this technique that Saints come into the world.
>
> *Light on Sant Mat*,
> Maharaj Charan Singh

It would seem then that, after all, the life of a mystic is vastly more practical than that of the materialist. If one wishes to put this to the test, he does not have to change his religion. But he is wise to ask himself if it is conveying him to the place he desires. All religions are part of the world's ethical structure, but Sant Mat practice allows true spiritual growth through direct experiences that progressively disclose one's true nature and reunite him with the Beloved.

This book or any other—be it a holy book or commentary or any sermon or lecture—is of necessity but a written or spoken symbol of the inner truths. The seeker on the threshold must eventually say, "Enough! Enough! These are but words and more words. Let me listen to what is said after the full stop." Silence is a thousand times more eloquent:

> ...When you talk with the Master inside, you do not speak with the tongue or lips nor hear with the ears.... It is a sort of understanding (soul to soul) rather than hearing with the ears; hence the sense of the words automatically passing from one to the other....
>
> If you do not find...any reference to [some of the inner experiences you have had] in books, it does not matter. Experience is something higher, and all the experiences cannot be put into books.
>
> *Light on Sant Mat*,
> Maharaj Charan Singh

That same seeker on the threshold should find, in the promise of the Sant Mat Masters, all the encouragement he needs to take the first step forward:

> There are no failures in Sant Mat. Sooner or later, the soul that is keeping its contact with the Sound Current will reach its Home. When the way to the Home is known, and one keeps the way, where is the room for doubt that Home will be reached?
>
> *Spiritual Gems*,
> Maharaj Sawan Singh

EPILOGUE

THE STORY OF THE RICH MERCHANT

Very early one morning, to the utter astonishment of myself and the alarm of my wife, I awoke to find myself sobbing unrestrainedly. Such a thing had never happened to me before, and to my wife's anxious inquiries, the story of the rich merchant came tumbling from my lips as related here. Indeed, I could not have retained it within myself, so clear and urgent was it in every detail, and the telling of it gave a great and soothing satisfaction deep within.

At the time, no special significance was attached to it in our minds except as a curious experience. It was some six years later that it arose once more with startling stereoscopic clarity as my own allegorical story, covering several incarnations.

As they say in the East, there is a story. Shall I tell you a story? Then, *mere dost* (my friend), be pleased to sit and I will not waste your valuable time. The story is about a merchant who had a big house in the country called Sant Mat, which is fed by five rivers. These rivers receive their water from the snows of the mountains, which are not so many miles away to the north.

This man, as I said, was a rich man, but he was also a busy man. He had many thousands of rupees and much merchandise, and his mind was much taken up with these things. He also loved a gay life, so that he had many visitors at his house when he was home, but he also spent much time away from home.

One night, it so happened that this man was at home, and he was feeling far from well. This was doubtless from eating too many rich foods and from having too many late nights. This night as he lay awake, restless on his bed, he heard a far off sound. It seemed to be someone singing a song, a very pathetic song. It persisted and would not let him rest, and he now recollected that he had heard this same sound many times before but had not paid any attention to it.

With this pathetic sound disturbing him deeply, there was nothing he could do but try to find out where it came from and why it was so sad. So he left his room and followed the sound.

As I have said, his house was very large; so large that he rarely used more than a small portion of it. Quietly he made his way in the darkness up the stairs to the attic rooms. The singing became louder as he went, and at the door of one room he stopped to listen, for this was clearly the source.

He quietly pushed open the door, and a strange sight met his eyes. The room was nearly dark, but there was light enough for him to see a small person sitting alone singing as he swayed slightly from side to side. The merchant thought, who could this strange person be? He was perhaps young but very pale and thin, a pathetic sight.

The merchant must have made some small noise, for the singing stopped, and two large frightened eyes looked at him. So surprised was he, and startled, that he quickly withdrew, shutting the door behind him.

He slept but little that night, and in the morning he inquired anxiously of his servant who the strange person in the attic was who sang so pathetically and was so ill-fed. His servant was not willing to speak, but when pressed to do so, he said, "Have you forgotten, master, that many years ago when you were establishing your trade and your friendship with the big merchants, you were upset by your baby brother, Meri Surat (my soul). He displeased you so much with his simple baby sayings that you were ashamed of him before your friends. You commanded that he be sent away so that you should not be further embarrassed. But, master, I hoped that one day you would need him; so greatly daring, I kept him far away in the attic. There he pines for his release and spends his days sadly singing."

Hearing this dreadful thing, the merchant was so distressed that he fled from his house and did not stop until he found himself outside of town. Here he sat upon a fallen tree to rest and console himself. A beggar who was also by chance sitting upon that same tree asked him, "Why do you grieve, master? Are you ill or have you lost money? What causes you to behave this way?"

The merchant, feeling fortunate to have someone to talk to, told the beggar the whole story. Then he said, "I must go to him. I must bathe him and give him my finest clothes, and I will ask all my friends to a banquet so that he may have everything that I have for myself."

The beggar said, "Oh, master! Would you be a still greater fool and add more suffering for both of you? Did you not see he was afraid of you? Do you not know he is unused to rich food and to rough merchants' talk? Would you kill him with your foolishness?"

The merchant said, "What should I do then? I cannot sleep again for anguish. If I cannot see my brother, of what use is my wealth?"

"Listen, master, and I will tell you what to do. First, take my garment and put it on. Then you will go to him in your humility and the Lord will cause you to cry. Your brother will not be frightened, and his heart is large. He will embrace you, and you will bathe him with your tears. Do not take him to your lavish apartments or to your rich banquets. You must come to him and feed him with tiny portions of your love."

And so it happened, just as the beggar said. Each day the merchant waited impatiently for evening to come. Then he put on the beggar's garment and went to Meri Surat, but he did not disclose that he was his brother for fear of angering him.

Then one day, feeling a deep love growing between them, he said that they must go away and travel together. "But where?" said the timid Meri Surat.

"I have heard of a wonderful country called Sach Khand, where we can be united in our new love forever."

"That would be wonderful my dear friend." (Meri Surat still did not know it was his brother.) "I am ready to accompany you."

"Then we will go. But first we must visit a great guru I have heard of. He will tell us the places we must stay and the places we should avoid, for I am told he has many times made this journey. And where he can go, perhaps by his grace we may also go."

So the merchant in beggar's clothing and Meri Surat left the big house by a side door, and close together, set off for the home of the Satguru.

That, my friend, is the end of the story. But you wish to know what happened to the two travellers to Sach Khand? That I cannot tell you. But as it happened, sometime afterwards I was greatly fortunate to be in the house of the Satguru, and I asked him if the two brothers had journeyed well together and what their adventures had been.

Maharaj Ji did not answer me directly. He folded my hands in his and said very quietly with a smile, "It's all right."

INFORMATION AND BOOKS ARE AVAILABLE FROM:

The Secretary
Radha Soami Satsang Beas
P.O. Dera Baba Jaimal Singh 143204
District Amritsar, Punjab, India

CANADA

Dr. J. Khanna, 5550 McMaster Road, Vancouver V6T 1J8, B. C.

Dr. Peter Grayson, 177 Division Street S.Kingsville, Ontario, N9Y 1R1, Canada

U.S.A.

Dr. Vincent Savarese, 3507 St. Elizabeth Rd., Glendale, CA 91206

Dr. Gene Ivash, 4701 Shadow Lane, Austin, TX 78731

Mr. Roy Ricks, 651 Davis St., Melrose Park, IL 60160

Dr. John Templer, 114 Verdier Rd., Beaufort, SC 29902

Dr. Frank Vogel, 7 Pelham Terrace, Arlington, MA 02174

MEXICO

Mr. Jorge Angel Santana, Cameta 2821, Jardines Del Bosque, Guadalajara, Jalisco

SOUTH AMERICA

Dr. Gonzalo Vargas N., P.O. Box 2666, Quito, Ecuador

Mr. Leopoldo Luks, Ave. Maracay, Urb. Las Palmas, Qta. Luksenburg, Caracas, Venezuela

Mrs. Rajni B. Manglani, % Bhagwan's Store, 18 Water Street, Georgetown, Guyana

WEST INDIES

Mr. Thakurdas Chatlani, 2A Gittins Avenue, Maraval, Trinidad

Mr. Sean Finnegan, P.O. Box 2314, Port-au-Prince, Haiti

Mr. Bhagwandas Kessaram, % Kiddies Corner, Swan Street, Bridgetown, Barbados

ENGLAND
Mrs. F.E. Wood, c/o Lloyd's Bank, 20 North Street, Leatherhead, Surrey.

SWEDEN
Mr. Lennart Zachen, Vintergatan, 15 A I, 172 30 Sundbyberg.

DENMARK
Ms. Inge Gregersen, Askevenget–15, 2830 Virum

HOLLAND
Mr. Jacob Hofstra, Geulwijk 6, 3831 LM Leusden

WEST GERMANY
Mr. Rudolf Walberg, Falkenstr. 18, D–6232 Bad Soden/Taunus

AUSTRIA
Mr. Hansjorg Hammerer, Sezenweingasse 10, A–5020, Salzburg

SWITZERLAND
Mr. Olivier de Coulon, Route de Lully, 1111 Tolochenaz

FRANCE
Count Pierre de Proyart, 7 Quai Voltaire, 75007 Paris

SPAIN
Mr. H. W. Balani, Balani's International, P.O. Box 486, Malaga

PORTUGAL
Mr. Alberto C. Ferreira, R. Machado dos Santos 20, 2775 Parede

GIBRALTAR
Mr. Arjan M. Thadani, Radha Soami Satsang Beas, P.O. Box 283

ITALY
Mr. Ted Goodman, Via Garigliano 27, Rome 00198

GREECE
Dr. Constantine Siopoulos, Thrakis 7, 145 61 Kifissia

CYPRUS
Mr. Hercules Achilleos, Kyriakou Matsi 18, Pallouriotissa—T. K. 9077, Nicosia

WEST AFRICA

Mr. Krishin Vaswani, Vaan-Ahn Enterprise Ltd., P.O. Box 507, Monrovia, Liberia

Mr. Nanik N. Balani, Kewalram (Nig.) Ltd., P.O. Box 320, Lagos, Nigeria

Mr. J.O.K. Sekyi, P.O. Box 4615, Accra, Ghana

EAST AFRICA

Mr. Sylvester Kakooza, P.O. Box 31381, Kampala, Uganda

Mr. Sohan Singh Bharj, P.O. Box 47036, Nairobi, Kenya

Mr. D. N. Pandit, United Timber Traders Ltd., P.O. Box 1963, Dar-es-Salaam, Tanzania

Mr. David Bowskill, P.O. Box 11012, Chingola, Zambia

Mr. Vernon Lowrie, P.O. Box 690, Harare, Zimbabwe

SOUTH AFRICA

Mr. Sam Busa, P.O. Box 41355, Craighall, Transvaal 2024

Mr. R. Attwell, P.O. Box 5702, Durban 4000

MASCARENE ISLANDS

Mr. D. S. Sumboo, 9 Bis Harris Street, Port Louis, Mauritius

ISRAEL

Mrs. H. Mandelbaum, P.O. Box 2815, Tel Aviv–61000

U. A. E.

Mr. Jiwatram Lakhiani, P.O. Box 1449. Dubai

KUWAIT

Mr. & Mrs. Ghassan Alghanem, P.O. Box 25549, 13116, Safat, Kuwait

AFGHANISTAN

Mr. Manak Singh, ℅ Manaco, P.O. Box 3163, Kabul

SRI LANKA

Mr. D. H. Jiwat, Geekay Ltd., 33 Bankshall Street, Colombo–11

NEW ZEALAND

Mr. Tony Waddicor, P.O. Box 5331, Wellesley St. P.O., Auckland 1

AUSTRALIA

Mrs. Janet Bland, P O. Box 3, Oaklands Park, South Australia 5046.

Mr. A.J. Walker, 8 445, Canning Highway, Melville, Western Australia 6156

INDONESIA
Mr. G. L. Nanwani, Yayasan, Radhasoami Satsang Beas,
JL. Kelinci Raya No. 32A, Jakarta Pusat
Mr. Bhagwan N. Chugani, % Jl. Coklat 20–22, Surabaya

SINGAPORE
Mr. Bhagwan Asnani, 1806 King's Mansion, Singapore–1543

MALAYSIA
Mr. N. Pal, % Muhibbah Travels Agency, Sdn. Bhd.,
46 Jalan Tanku Abdul Rahman, Kuala Lumpur 01–07

THAILAND
Mr. Harmahinder Singh Sethi, Sawan Textiles Ltd.,
154 Serm Sin Kha, Sampheng, Bangkok-10100

HONG KONG
Mrs. Cami Moss, Hongkong Hilton, G.P.O. Box 42
Mr. Gobind Sabnani, G.P.O. Box 3906

PHILIPPINES
Mr. Kay Sham, P.O. Box 2346 MCC, Makati, Metro Manila

JAPAN
Mr. L. H. Parwani, Radha Soami Satsang Beas, 2–18 Nakajimadori
1–Chome, Aotani, Fukiai-ku, Kobe–651

* * * * * * * *

FOR OTHER FOREIGN ORDERS WRITE TO:
Mr. Krishin Babani, Buona Casa Bldg., 2nd Floor, Sir P. M. Road,
Fort Bombay–400 001, India

Addresses changed since this book was printed:

BOOKS ON THIS SCIENCE

Soami Ji Maharaj

1. *Sar Bachan*

Baba Jaimal Singh

2. *Spiritual Letters* (to Huzur Maharaj Sawan Singh: 1896–1903)

Huzur Maharaj Sawan Singh

3. *Discourses on Sant Mat*
4. *Philosophy of the Masters (Gurmat Sidhant)*, 5 vols. (an encyclopedia on the teachings of the Saints)
5. *My Submission* (introduction to *Philosophy of the Masters*)
6. *Philosophy of the Masters* (abridged)
7. *Tales of the Mystic East* (as narrated in satsangs)
8. *Spiritual Gems* (letters: 1919–1948)
9. *The Dawn of Light* (letters: 1911–1934)

Sardar Bahadur Jagat Singh Maharaj

10. *The Science of the Soul* (discourses and letters: 1948–1951)

Maharaj Charan Singh

11. *Die to Live* (answers to questions on meditation)
12. *Divine Light* (discourses and letters: 1959–1964)
13. *The Path* (first part of *Divine Light*)
14. *Light on Saint Matthew*
15. *Light on Sant Mat* (discourses and letters: 1952–1958)
16. *Quest for Light* (letters: 1965–1971)
17. *Light on Saint John*
18. *Spiritual Discourses*
19. *Spiritual Heritage* (from tape-recorded talks)
20. *The Master Answers* (to audiences in America: 1964)
21. *Thus Saith the Master* (to audiences in America: 1970)
22. *Truth Eternal* (a discourse)

Books about the Masters

1. *Call of the Great Master*—Diwan Daryai Lal Kapur
2. *The Living Master*—Katherine Wason
3. *With a Great Master in India*—Dr. Julian P. Johnson
4. *With the Three Masters*, 3 vols.—from the diary of Rai Sahib Munshi Ram
5. *Heaven On Earth*—Diwan Daryai Lal Kapur

Books on Sant Mat in general

1. *A Soul's Safari*—Netta Pfeifer
2. *In Search of the Way*—Flora E. Wood
3. *Kabir, The Great Mystic*—Isaac A. Ezekiel
4. *Liberation of the Soul*—J. Stanley White, Ph.D.
5. *Message Divine*—Shanti Sethi
6. *Mystic Bible*—Dr. Randolph Stone
7. *Mysticism, The Spiritual Path*, 2 vols.—Prof. Lekh Raj Puri
8. *Radha Soami Teachings*—Prof. Lekh Raj Puri
9. *Ringing Radiance*—Sir Colin Garbett
10. *Sant Mat and the Bible*—Narain Das
11. *Sarmad, Jewish Saint of India*—Isaac A. Ezekiel
12. *Teachings of the Gurus*—Prof. Lekh Raj Puri
13. *The Inner Voice*—Colonel C. W. Sanders
14. *The Mystic Philosophy of Sant Mat*—Peter Fripp
15. *The Path of the Masters*—Dr. Julian P. Johnson
16. *Yoga and the Bible*—Joseph Leeming

Mystics of the East Series

1. *Saint Paltu*—Isaac A. Ezekiel
2. *Saint Namdev, His Life and Teachings*—J. R. Puri and V. K. Sethi
3. *Tulsi Sahib, Saint of Hathras*—J. R. Puri and V. K. Sethi
4. *Tukaram, Saint of Maharashtra*—C. Rajwade
5. *Dadu, The Compassionate Mystic*—K. N. Upadhyaya, Ph.D.
6. *Mira, The Divine Lover*—V. K. Sethi
7. *Guru Ravidas, Life and Teachings*—K. N. Upadhyaya, Ph.D.
8. *Guru Nanak, His Mystic Teachings*—J. R. Puri
9. *Kabir, The Weaver of God's Name*—V. K. Sethi
10. *Bulleh Shah* J.R Puri and T.R. Shangari
11. *Dariya Sahib, Saint of Bihar*—K. N. Upadhyaya, Ph.D.